MAKE THE
IMPOSSIBLE
POSSIBLE

MAKE THE
IMPOSSIBLE
POSSIBLE

One Man's Crusade to
Inspire Others to Dream Bigger
and Achieve the

EXTRAORDINARY

BILL STRICKLAND
with Vince Rause

CURRENCY / DOUBLEDAY
New York London Toronto Sydney Auckland

To the life and spirit of my mother
Evelyn Strickland

A CURRENCY BOOK
PUBLISHED BY DOUBLEDAY

Published in the United States by Doubleday, an imprint of The Doubleday Broadway Publishing Group, a division of Random House, Inc., New York.
www.currencybooks.com

Book design by Chris Welch

Library of Congress Cataloging-in-Publication Data

Strickland, Bill, 1947–
Make the impossible possible : one man's crusade to inspire others to dream bigger and achieve the extraordinary / by Bill Strickland, with Vince Rause.—1st ed.
p.   cm.
Includes index.
1. Strickland, Bill, 1947– 2. Self-actualization (Psychology)
I. Rause, Vince. II. Title.

BF637.S4S828 2007
650.1—dc22

2007027827

ISBN 978-0-385-52054-6

PRINTED IN THE UNITED STATES OF AMERICA

SPECIAL SALES
Currency Books are available at special discounts for bulk purchases for sales promotions or premiums. Special editions, including personalized covers, excerpts of existing books, and corporate imprints, can be created in large quantities for special needs. For more information, write to Special Markets, Currency Books, specialmarkets@randomhouse.com

1 3 5 7 9 10 8 6 4 2
First Edition

CONTENTS

CHAPTER ONE From the Ghetto to Harvard Business School 1

CHAPTER TWO Growing Up 28

CHAPTER THREE A Dream Is Born 50

CHAPTER FOUR Expanding Our Mission 72

CHAPTER FIVE The Secret to Success 102

CHAPTER SIX Impossibility Thinking 128

CHAPTER SEVEN The Power of Passion 147

CHAPTER EIGHT Swing 172

CHAPTER NINE Reach 193

CHAPTER TEN Purpose 219

Index 229

MAKE THE
IMPOSSIBLE
POSSIBLE

To Ann,
Great to meet
you at your book
club.

Warmest Regards,

Vince Roehse

CHAPTER ONE

From the Ghetto to Harvard Business School

I t was a winter morning in 1996 and I was standing center stage in the pit of a jam-packed, wood-paneled lecture hall at Harvard University. Rows of wooden seats loomed above me in curving tiers. In those seats, with their expectant gazes bearing down on me, sat about one hundred razor-sharp young men and women—graduate students at the Harvard Business School—waiting to see what I had to offer. As a result of my work with inner-city kids and adults at the Manchester Bidwell Center in Pittsburgh, I had been asked to serve as an HBS case study, to share a little hard-earned business savvy from the other side of the tracks.

As Professor Jim Heskett introduced me to his class, I positioned my beat-up old slide projector on a tabletop, then opened a battered cardboard box, held together with duct tape at the corners, and lifted out a loaded carousel of slides. The students looked me over. In recent weeks, such other speakers as Disney honcho Michael Eisner and Southwest Airlines chief Herb Kelleher had stood where I was standing to share their business philosophies and reveal their secrets of success. Now it was my turn in the spotlight. I knew the kids weren't sure what to expect from me. To tell the truth, I wasn't so sure that they could get what I had to offer. After all, I don't run an airline or an entertainment empire. If you wanted to be technical about it, you could say I'm not a businessman at all. As the founder and CEO of Manchester Bidwell, a community arts-education and job-training center in Pittsburgh, my mission is to turn people's lives around. We do that by offering them two distinct educational programs under the same roof. The first program, which we call the Manchester Craftsmen's Guild, offers rigorous after-school courses in the arts that light a creative fire in at-risk kids and inspire them to stay in school. Classes at the Craftsmen's Guild are taught by a staff of established artists and skilled instructors, and the curriculum is designed to rival courses taught at the best private schools and academies. Our center also houses the Bidwell Training Center, which provides state-of-the-art job-training programs intended to give poor and otherwise disadvantaged adults the skills and direction they need to land meaningful, good-paying jobs that provide the foundation for a much brighter future. Our students include welfare mothers, recovering addicts, ex-convicts, laid-off manufacturing workers, and others who have had hope or even dignity snatched away by the difficult circumstances of their lives. Our younger students at the Craftsmen's Guild face similar struggles. Many of them are on a fast track to failure when they come to us, flunking courses, skipping school, on the verge of dropping out or being suspended. Some of them swagger in, angry, defiant, bristling with hostile attitude. Others hide behind a prickly shell of apathy and withdrawal.

When we started out some twenty years ago, most of our students were African-Americans from the city's poorest neighborhoods. Today, almost half our student body is made up of disadvantaged white folks. We greet them all with the same basic recipe for success: high standards, stiff challenges, a chance to develop unexplored talents, and a message that many of them haven't heard before—that no matter how difficult the circumstances of their lives may be, no matter how many bad assumptions they've made about their chances in life, no matter how well they've been taught to rein in their dreams and narrow their aspirations, they have the right, and the potential, to expect to live rich and satisfying lives. It takes some time for them to adjust to that message and trust our faith in their potential, but once they do, the transformation is remarkable, and our success rates, compiled over more than twenty years, show that we must be doing something right.

More than 90 percent of the kids who come to us get their high school diplomas and 85 percent enroll in college or some other form of higher education. Our job-training programs for disadvantaged adults are yielding similar successes: Almost 80 percent of our adult students complete their vocational training and 86 percent of them find employment after graduation. And I'm not talking about flipping burgers. These are good, substantial jobs—as sous chefs, chemical and pharmaceutical technicians, and the like—jobs that can lift an entire family out of poverty and personal inertia, and offer a real chance at a stable and rewarding future.

The success of Manchester Bidwell has won us a lot of respect and support from the business community across the country, and it has helped us forge dynamic corporate partnerships with companies like IBM, Alcoa, PPG Industries, Heinz, Hewlett-Packard, Bayer,

Mylan Labs, Nova Chemicals, and many more. Leading figures in politics, education, and the arts have also singled us out for praise (we're one of very few programs, I'm sure, ever to draw the enthusiastic support of both Hillary Clinton and prominent conservative Rick Santorum, the former U.S. senator from Pennsylvania), and our work here has brought me a humbling litany of honors and personal recognition. I've been appointed to the National Council on the Arts, the National Endowment for the Arts, and the President's Committee on the Arts and Humanities. Two presidents have summoned me to the White House to discuss our operations, and ten universities have awarded me honorary Ph.D.'s. In 1999, the MacArthur Foundation gave me one of their famous "genius grants," and I am now a trustee at the University of Pittsburgh, the school that had to be coaxed to accept me as a probationary student thirty-four years ago. Along with my staff, I've also received some remarkable attention from the world of music in recognition of the jazz program that has evolved at the center as part of the innovative mix that gives the place its creative spirit. Since 1987, Manchester Bidwell has hosted a live jazz concert series, which draws the top jazz artists in the world to perform here, in the intimate music hall that is part of our facility. Our music program, one of the oldest and most successful jazz subscription series in the country, has made Manchester Bidwell one of the most highly regarded jazz venues in the nation, and it has also spawned our own recording label—MCG Jazz—which produces and distributes jazz albums by some of the premier jazz artists on the planet, including Nancy Wilson, The Count Basie Orchestra, the New York Voices, and Brazilian superstar Ivan Lins. The quality of our recordings has been validated again and again by the music industry: Seven of our releases have been nominated for Grammy Awards in various jazz categories, and four of those nominated albums brought Grammys home to Manchester.

All this unlikely and unexpected recognition has created an ever-widening ripple of interest in our operations, and for years I've been crisscrossing the country, sharing the Manchester Bidwell story with anyone who will listen—at conferences and seminars everywhere, with audiences that include influential leaders in the fields of business, education, government, and the arts, from laid-back, denim-clad technology tycoons in the Silicon Valley to the prim and pious parishioners of evangelist Robert Schuller's Crystal Cathedral.

I welcome this attention, because it means people are noticing that we are doing something special at Manchester Bidwell, acknowledging that our success here has something to say not only to the disadvantaged people we serve at the school but to people everywhere, from all walks of life. Still, on a personal level, as a guy who never forgot where he came from, and who knows firsthand how the realities of race and circumstance, poverty and lowered expectations, can crush human dreams, it amazes me more than a little. I was certainly amazed when Jim Heskett at Harvard got interested in our work. He was intrigued with the news of our success and with the unconventional methods we use, and thought his students might learn something from the way I operate. So he decided to make Manchester Bidwell the subject of a Harvard case study, an extensive, intensive business analysis of what we do and how we do it. Over the next few months, his students studied every aspect of our organization with the same hard-boiled scrutiny they'd bring to bear if we were a software giant or cell phone manufacturer instead of an organization dedicated to shaping and guiding the human spirit. Then Jim invited me to his class to answer his students' questions and offer whatever wisdom I'd gathered from my long years in the trenches. Or something like that. To be honest, as I stood there in the lecture pit that winter morning I wasn't really sure what Jim wanted from me. But one thing was certain: He wasn't expecting me to spout a lot of conventional business wisdom; he knew enough about my story to understand that I don't have much of that. I'm no textbook CEO. I don't have an M.B.A. Never took a business course in my life. The truth is, I never set out to be a corporate executive or to run any kind of operation at all. When I started out, all I wanted was to give some kids a chance to work with clay.

I was nineteen years old in 1968 when I founded the Manchester Craftsmen's Guild, the tiny neighborhood arts center that grew into Manchester Bidwell. Our first home was a derelict row house on Buena Vista Street in Manchester. My plan was to use the space as a studio where I could teach neighborhood kids to make bowls and pots. I was a neophyte potter myself at the time, and making pottery was one of the great joys of my life. I liked the way the wet clay felt in my hands. Working with clay calmed me and excited me all at the same time. There was a sense of control, but also one of rich possibility. And there was a potent sense of accomplishment and pride once you developed some skill at it. A high school art teacher had turned me on to the craft and has been my hero ever since. I was just another aimless kid, coasting through school, bored and disengaged, with no sense of what I'd do with my life after graduation, when Frank Ross invited me into his classroom and let me sit at his potter's wheel. The magic I felt when I first laid my hands on wet clay gave me the belief that I could do something interesting with my life. It opened up doors to meaning and possibility that showed me, for the first time, that I had talents and capabilities no one had seen before and that I had never dreamed of. I'm convinced that those insights not only gave me a vision of my future, they literally saved my life.

In 1968, Manchester was suffering from the racial strife that rocked so many inner-city neighborhoods in the wake of the assassination of Martin Luther King Jr. Homes were in flames, riot cops and armed National Guard troops patrolled the streets, there were shootings and frequent clashes between demonstrators and police, and in the middle of it all were a lot of terrified kids, wondering if someone was going to shoot them or set their house on fire.

I wanted to do something for those kids, but I had no experience as a social worker, teacher, or community activist. I was a know-nothing freshman at the University of Pittsburgh at the time, trying my best to keep from flunking out and to get my own life in order. All I knew was clay and what it had done for me. Intuitively, I knew it could do the same for them. I knew what they needed—a safe, sane, quiet environment where they could escape the madness that reigned in the streets, work on some clay, find a way to shape something personal and beautiful, and spend some time in a bright, clean, nurturing place where it did not seem pointless to dream. With the help of local Episcopalian churches, I was able to secure a ramshackle row house, which I cleaned and painted, then furnished with potter's wheels and stocked with clay.

Then I christened the place the Manchester Craftsmen's Guild and opened the doors. Curious kids trickled in off the sidewalks to see what I was up to. I taught them how to use the wheels, how to center and shape the clay. I don't know what I thought would happen. On some level, I knew I needed such a place as much as the kids did—a place where I could keep believing in the power of my own creative possibilities despite the darkness closing in all around me—and I hoped the place would shield them from all the poison that was in the streets. At first it was enough just to see them being kids again, giggling each time one of their wobbly pots collapsed into a slippery lump. But some of them kept coming back. I worked with them until they could get the clay to rise and hold form, then work it carefully into a shape that would please the eye. It was an amazing thing to see the looks on their faces as they worked—the concentration, the sense of purpose and power, and the sudden glint of excitement as they watched the clay morph into the very pot they had pictured in their minds. I knew what that felt like—like you had the whole world in your hands. That was the magic I wanted them to feel. And I knew that, for those moments at least, the troubles of Manchester were far away.

From the start, I loved the work I was doing, the feeling it gave me to help others open their eyes and see the possibilities before them. But I had no long-term vision for the Craftsmen's Guild. I saw it as a stopgap measure, a life raft for those kids. I certainly never thought it would lead to my life's work. My plan was to get my education degree, then teach history to high school students. But life takes some odd twists and turns. I started hearing from teachers in nearby public schools. They noticed that the kids who came to the Craftsmen's Guild were showing up at school more often. They were behaving better in the classroom, too. And their grades were starting to improve.

That drew people's attention. Word soon got around that something interesting was happening on Buena Vista Street. Neighborhood leaders began to mark me as a guy who was doing some good in the community. Local artists lent us their support. I was introduced to all the right people, and sources of funding appeared before my eyes. I hired a staff and added programs. More kids walked through the door. The place was taking on a life and an energy of its own, growing rapidly in size, in complexity, and in the scope of its missions. I had no choice but to grow with it. And that meant developing my leadership and management skills, often on the fly.

Thirty-four years later, the center and I are both still growing, but in a much larger and more sophisticated facility. Today, Manchester Bidwell comprises three separate buildings covering 163,000 square feet, with 150 people on staff and some 1,200 students passing through our doors each year, not counting the 2,500 young people served by the programs we operate in public school classrooms as a cooperative venture with the Pittsburgh school district. Running such a complex organization requires a pretty high level of organizational expertise, and today I feel very comfortable wearing the hat of CEO. But I'll never forget that Manchester Bidwell wasn't crafted out of corporate vision or business savvy. It happened because a clueless nineteen year old trusted his unspoken intuition that the human spirit is remarkably resilient, and that even in damaged and disadvantaged lives, and in circumstances where the odds seem hopelessly stacked against you, there is endless potential waiting to be freed. What I wanted those Harvard grad students to understand, what I want everyone who reads this book to embrace, are the simple principles that have guided my life and enabled my success: that all of us have the potential to make our dreams come true, and that one of the greatest obstacles blocking us from realizing that potential is that we

believe, or are told, the things we want most passionately are impractical, unrealistic, or somehow beyond our reach. The story I have to
share with you is the story of the pursuit of one unrealistic, impractical, outrageous dream after another, and the remarkable consistency
with which those dreams have come true. That didn't happen by
magic. It happened because I refused to be limited by what conventional wisdom, or other people, or the cautious little voice we all have
in our heads told me I couldn't do. I haven't accomplished everything
I set out to do, but I've accomplished a whole lot more than I would
have if I'd let myself be boxed in by common sense and "sensible" expectations. To put it in simplest terms, I left the door open to possibility and, more often than not, opportunity showed its face. They gave
me a genius award for thinking like that, but it's nothing any clear-
thinking person can't manage. Each one of us, no matter who our parents are, where we live, how much education we have, or what kinds
of connections, abilities, and opportunities life may have offered us,
has the potential to shape our lives in ways that will bring us the
meaning, purpose, and success we long for. That's the essential lesson
of my life and of this book: that each of us can achieve the "impossible" in our lives. I want everyone who comes to this book, no matter
what their age or accomplishments or the circumstances of their lives,
to rethink their assumptions about what is and isn't possible in their
lives, and to convince themselves that they have not only the right but
also the responsibility, and the capacity, to dream big and to make
those dreams come true.

As I stood at the podium facing those bright-eyed Harvard students, I knew that before I could convey the message I'd come to share

with them, I'd have to overcome some assumptions that people commonly make about me. For example, many people immediately size me up as a guru type, an urban do-gooder who has devoted his life to selflessly helping the poor. In fact, I have dedicated my life to helping other people, and I'm proud of what I've accomplished along those lines, but you can't really understand me, or what my life has been about, unless you grasp the fact that I didn't do any of it out of *selflessness*. I did it to be *myself*. I did it to enrich my own life, to deepen the quality and meaning of my own experience. I did it because it was a part of what I had to do if I genuinely wanted to be *me*. If the MacArthur people are right, if I have even a small shred of genius in my soul, it's only because I have an unshakable belief that each of us has not only the potential to live a rewarding and purposeful life but also the *responsibility* to do so. It's an obligation we bear as human beings, but it's also the source of our greatest potential. Owning up to that obligation not only makes us more human, it also connects us to the bottomless reserves of passion, vision, conviction, and commitment that I believe are present in abundance in every human heart, and that are the fuel for genuine and deeply fulfilling success.

I wasn't about to give those students a lecture on altruism, activism, or any other -ism; I wasn't there to convince them they should commit their lives to others. I had a more radical notion to share with them, a new definition of success. I wanted them to understand that success isn't a destination. It's not something you pursue like a racetrack greyhound chasing a mechanical rabbit. Success is something you assemble from components you discover in your soul and your imagination. Authentic success, the kind of success that will enrich your life and enlarge your spirit, the only kind of success that matters, comes from knowing and trusting the deepest aspirations of your heart. If you try to live that way, in harmony with the real needs of your spirit, then you can't help but craft a life that will automatically make the world a better place for everyone who lives in it, and, incidentally, you will dramatically increase your chances for success on all levels. That's the insight I most wanted those Harvard kids to hear, but I knew mere words wouldn't carry enough weight—they didn't know me well enough. So I asked Jim Heskett to turn down the lights and I started to show my slides.

"Here is the place I built," I said as an image of the Manchester Bidwell Center flashed onto the screen. I could tell it wasn't what they expected. The image was an exterior shot, taken at night, of a sleek and striking contemporary structure. Low-slung, inviting, and subtle, the center has walls of adobe-colored block. Golden light glowed in the tall picture windows and rooftop canopies; a floodlit fountain sat at the center of a courtyard. "This building was created by the same architect who designed the Pittsburgh International Airport," I explained. "He was a student of Frank Lloyd Wright—a hero of mine— and I think he captured some of the magic of the master's touch. As a kid I'd spend hours looking at these kinds of buildings in books and architecture magazines. I wanted our kids to feel they deserved to study in such a building, and now I go to work in one every day."

The next slide took them inside the center. The soaring lobby, done in more of the earth-toned block, was flooded with light from banks of tall windows. Accents of natural wood brightened the space, and intimately arched alcoves led the way to quiet halls. I pointed out the small touches—the rich carpets, the designer tile, the handmade stained-glass inserts in the office doors, the bouquets of fresh flowers. "This place is my idea of a perfect human shelter," I said. "It generates order and serenity and stability and optimism, things many of our students do not enjoy in abundance in their private lives. Poor people live in a world where beauty seems impossible. We make it possible. Then the world and eventually the future look very different to them."

The screen lit up with an image of a brilliantly colored "story cloth" woven by members of Pittsburgh's Hmong community. For centuries, the Hmong, from Southeast Asia, had no written language, so they created visual narratives of their history and legends on their exquisitely crafted works of cloth. "Hmong artists made these cloths especially for us," I explained, "and now these wonderful pieces, reflecting an image of beauty crafted in a culture thousands of miles away, are part of their everyday lives."

The next slide showed a massive bench, crafted in a rustic Japanese style from a single slab of thick, hand-hewn red oak resting on two sturdy posts. "I had a young Japanese guy working for me as a carpenter. I found out he was also a furniture maker who had studied under the great George Nakashima. So I had him build me this bench. He's a successful furniture maker now and his pieces cost a small fortune. But before he left he built some sixty pieces just for us—all one-of-a-kind works of art, for all the public spaces. Now, when welfare mothers come into our place, tired from the couple of bus rides it took to get here, they find themselves resting on pieces of art. I want our students to get comfortable with art. I want them to be confronted by something beautiful every time they turn around. So all our hallways and public spaces are graced with the works of fine artists from all over the world: woven tapestries, African-inspired sculpture, fine-art photographs."

Next, I brought up an image of the beautiful quilts that hang like tapestries on the tall walls of our main lobby. "These quilts cost a bundle," I said. "They were hand-made by a craft cooperative made up of mostly elderly ladies who live in a very rural part of Pennsylvania. They make these quilts in their homes, as a cottage industry, using the styles and principles of the Amish quilt makers who are their inspiration. Amish-style quilts might not be the first decorative element you think of when you're furnishing an educational center in the inner city, and I'm sure that none of the ladies in the cooperative had spent much time in a place like Manchester, but all I cared about was that the quilts these ladies produced were exceptional, and that they would add another layer of softness and beauty to my school. Still, I told them that I wouldn't give them the commission until they visited us in Pittsburgh and convinced me that they understood the spirit of the center. So one day they arrived in cars and pickups and walked inside, a group of very gentle-looking, very white little old ladies. I showed them around. At first they just gazed at the place, silent and wide-eyed. Our students were a little wide-eyed, too. These gentle country ladies couldn't have seemed more out of place if they had dropped into Manchester directly from the moon. But as soon as we started to talk about the quilts—about materials, patterns, themes, and colors—all the strangeness went away and we became just a bunch of people talking about art and the enterprise of making a beautiful thing. Our students couldn't help but see the passion those women had for their work, and all the things they needed to do that work well—the skills and vision to create a quilt that captures life and meaning and some measure of truth. They were the same things our students were struggling to master in their classes. With a flash of insight, they saw beyond the superficial differences that made our visitors so foreign to them. Instead, they saw fellow artists with whom they had a common bent.

"That's the power of art," I said to Jim Heskett's class. "Art is a bridge. It connects you to a wider world, to a broader experience. I don't expect a bunch of poor kids from the streets to become overnight aficionados because they see a pretty picture, but don't try to tell me that exposure to the arts doesn't have the power to change a human being. It gets in their bones, man. It gets in all of our bones—that is the power of the arts in our lives. I've seen it and its magic. Our students stop defining themselves by what they can't do and get the first glimmer of what a meaningful life might feel like.

"Speaking of magic," I added, "this is not some Manhattan art gallery, this is where our students showcase their work." The new slide showed a small but elegant exhibition space, enclosed by plate-glass walls and lit with crisp track lighting. "Can you imagine what it feels like to inner-city kids to have their work displayed in a setting like this?" I asked. "To have their efforts celebrated this way? We make a big deal about showing their art—there's always an opening night, we serve refreshments, a live jazz combo plays. The kids invite whomever they want and we always get a good crowd—relatives, neighbors, everyone from the school. It's a new experience for most of these kids to feel that kind of support and recognition, and my experience tells me it does wonders for their souls."

The new Manchester Bidwell Center stands just a few city blocks from Oliver High School, my old alma mater. At Oliver High, students are greeted each morning by security guards who inspect their backpacks and march them through metal detectors. The windows are protected with iron bars. To me, the place feels more like a jail than a school, so it's no surprise that so many students behave so badly there, vandalizing the place, disrespecting teachers and each other, and showing angry contempt for the process of learning. Administrators have installed all sorts of get-tough policies at Oliver, but the kids still run amok, and overwhelmed teachers often feel more like prison guards than educators. Many kids are afraid to walk the halls. Attendance is poor. The dropout rate is through the roof.

We don't have armed guards at Manchester Bidwell. Our students don't pass through metal detectors. We don't make them empty their pockets and we don't rummage through their bags. There are no security cameras keeping watch over our grounds. We feed our kids gourmet lunches prepared by students in our culinary program. We surround them with museum-quality art. We give them a place of sunlight and energy. The result is remarkable: Even though the neighborhood around us has one of the highest crime rates in the city, we have never, in all the years of our existence, had a single reason to call the police. There have been no thefts or burglaries, no violence, no vandalism. We've never had a car broken into, never had to scrub graffiti off a wall. The thing is, many of our students are the very same kids who have been branded as incorrigible or worse at Oliver High, and kids just like them from other schools across the city.

So why do they show our place such respect? Do they undergo some sort of biochemical change as they travel that short distance from Oliver to our place, some spontaneous realignment of their DNA? Or could it be that there's nothing fundamentally wrong with the kids? Could it be that they're only living up to the low expectations society holds for them and that they've been taught to hold for themselves? Is it possible, in fact, that poor folks of all ages, including our adult students at Bidwell, have spirits that, despite the ravages of poverty, still respond to and flourish in an environment that provides them with order, purpose, opportunity, and beauty? To me, the answer is clear: We show our students trust and they learn they can be trusted. We treat them with respect and get respectful behavior in return. We put them in a beautiful place, give them a small taste of what a decent, dignified future might feel like, and that makes all the difference. The beauty we've designed into our center isn't window dressing; it's an essential part of our success. It nourishes the spirit, and until you reach that part of the spirit that isn't touched by cynicism or despair, no change can begin. You can't show a person how to build a better life if they feel no pleasure in the simple act of being alive. That's why I built this place, and why I fill it with art, and sunlight, and quilts, and flowers. So some black kid who thinks the whole world is as stale and gray as the ghetto, or some white kid from some hardscrabble blue-collar neighborhood ravaged by layoffs and chronic underemployment, can find out what an orchid smells like. So when some poor single mother walks into our place, after hours at some miserable job, after scrambling to find someone to take care of her kids, after riding buses, bumming rides, or walking on her own two feet to get here, she gets to rest for a moment on an exquisitely made, one-of-a-kind Japanese bench handcrafted by a master craftsman just for her. How can she help but start thinking she deserves that beautiful bench? How can she stop herself from thinking she deserves even more beauty and order in her life? Small changes like that, small rich human experiences, are how you plant the seeds of a dream. You can't inspire a person to live a better life if they don't know what a good life feels like. Flowers, clay, art, and sunlit spaces don't work miracles, but they can set the stage on which miracles occur. At Manchester Bidwell, we see those kinds of miracles every day.

Once we had a student named Sharif Bey. When I first laid eyes on him, I thought, *This is going to be a tough one.* Like so many kids who come here, Sharif seemed bitterly withdrawn and uncommunicative when he arrived. He was a ninth grader, a skinny kid who drifted down the hallways like a shadow, with his shoulders slumped and his head bowed down. He spoke only in whispers and kept his gaze riveted on the floor. It seemed he didn't have it in him to look you in the eye.

After his orientation period, Sharif decided to enroll in our ceramics program. We have a bright, airy studio outfitted with state-of-the-art tools and equipment. Dozens of finished pieces, resting on shelves and racks, provide tangible examples of the rewards of hard work. The space is always buzzing with a soft, creative energy as kids move their pieces from the pottery wheels to the worktables and eventually to a room where they are fired in our kilns. Most of our students think of the studio as a magical place. But Sharif showed no signs of even noticing the space around him. On his first day in the studio he dragged a chair into a corner, slumped into it, and stared into space. He seemed to be ignoring his instructors and the other students, and was apparently immune to the creative activity all around him.

But you never know what's going on inside a kid's head, so when his instructors asked me what they should do with him, I said, "Just keep giving him clay." To be honest, I didn't have high hopes for the kid. His only chance, I knew, was that the nurturing environment he was surrounded by, and the creative vibe that filled the studio every day, would change him on some level none of us could see. Happily, that's exactly what happened. One day when he was finally ready, Sharif quietly loaded some clay on a wheel and began to work. What happened next was one of the many small miracles that keep me doing what I do: The kid turned out to be a natural. Everyone saw it right away. The technique came to him quickly. More important, he had the touch, he had a sense of proportion, he had an artist's eye for texture, color, and grace. In no time he was turning out beautiful pieces, getting better and better with each one. I knew what he was going through, because I had gone through it myself: He was getting his first taste of meaningful success, and success felt good to him, better than almost anything be had ever felt. He wanted more of that feeling, and he knew that in order to have it he would have to get better. So he opened up to the world. He sought out the help of his teachers. He brainstormed with other talented kids. He studied the work of established artists and experimented with the clay, eager to find his own style. Working with clay had given him a sense of purpose and direction. It had given him a passion to achieve. That passion helped transform him, and after a few months with us he seemed like a whole new kid. I remember seeing him in the studio one day, waiting for a piece he'd finished to be taken out of the kiln. For ceramic artists, removing a piece from the kiln is always an act of faith; so many things can go wrong while a piece is being fired. But Sharif was standing tall as he waited, smiling and chatting with friends, his face lit up with confidence and anticipation. I saw hope, humor, and enthusiasm in his eyes. It was the look of a kid who expects to succeed. When I saw that, I knew Sharif was going to be all right.

Sharif was with us for many years, and before he was finished he proved himself to be one of the best ceramics students we'd ever had. And we weren't the only people who thought so. In his senior year, Sharif received scholarship offers from the art departments of three different colleges. He eventually enrolled at Slippery Rock University, on a full scholarship, where he earned his B.A. with flying colors, then a master's degree in fine art. While in graduate school, his talent and academic achievement earned him a Fulbright Scholarship. With his M.F.A. in hand, he went on to Penn State, where be earned a Ph.D. in arts education. Today, Sharif is an assistant professor of fine arts at Winston-Salem State University, and director of that school's arts education program.

Recently, I heard from Sharif. "I might have looked uncommunicative, almost reclusive, when I showed up at the Craftsmen's Guild," he said, "but you have to understand, at that point in my life, I'd never even had a conversation with a white person. In the studio, my teachers were white, there were lots of white kids from neighborhoods I'd never been to. Some of them were from affluent families. Some of them were Ivy League bound. I didn't know what to expect from them. I wasn't sure how to behave. My teachers were telling me I was capable of more than I thought, and making it clear their expectations were very high. That was disorienting. I'd never had any context for interacting with people who treated me like that, or thought of their own lives that way. But the studio gave me the context, the clay gave me the context. It took me a while to get it, but eventually I saw that all the kids in the class—white, black, Asian, Hispanic, whether they were rich or poor—had moved beyond the superficial characteristics that made them different, and were relating to each other as fellow artists through the creative work they were doing. When I started working,

I shared that rapport. Suddenly I had something to talk to them about; differences became unimportant, as the art became a bridge that led me out of my narrow experience and opened up my world. Each success I enjoyed at the Manchester Craftsmen's Guild gave me reason to believe that more successes were possible. More than anything, it was that belief in my own potential that allowed me to build the life I lead today."

I'm immensely proud of Sharif's accomplishments, because his story captures, in an especially dramatic form, the kinds of successes we see at Manchester Bidwell all the time. Every time I think of him lecturing his classes, passing on his love for art and beauty to his students, I can't help thinking of that shy, skinny kid sitting in his chair in the corner, staring into space, and the remarkable distance that young man was able to travel once someone gave him reason to believe he could.

The slide show continued. I showed them shots of our sleek new digital arts lab, put together with expertise and state-of-the-art technology contributed by Hewlett-Packard, our world-class ceramics studio—the direct descendant of the original Craftsmen's Guild— and our professional-caliber photography facilities. "On the first day of the photography program, we give the kids an expensive camera," I explained. "Some of the kids can't believe it. Nobody ever trusted them like that before. They come in here hampered by certain assumptions about life, and by assumptions about the assumptions other people are making about them. But we hand them a camera, we show them our trust and high expectations, and just like that we get them to question some bad ideas that might be holding them back." The slide of the photo studio reminded me of another student whose transformation made a lasting impression on me. His name was Gabe Tait. I knew his father from the neighborhood. Gabe's older brother was in prison serving a life term for murder. On the day his old man brought him in, he said, "Bill, I lost one son to the streets; I don't want to lose another. See if you can help him." Gabe signed up for the photo program. At first, he gave us the usual too-cool-for-school persona, but when they handed him a camera and he held it in his hand, he couldn't hide his excitement. Like Sharif, Gabe had talent, and pursuing that talent soon became hipper, more enticing, and more important than any cheap thrill the streets could offer. Today, Gabe is an award-winning photojournalist who has worked for several major newspapers, including the *Detroit Free Press* and the *St. Louis Post-Dispatch*. Recently, Gabe left journalism to become a missionary in Africa, and now is helping poor people there learn some of the lessons he learned as a student at the Manchester Craftsmen's Guild. There are lots of stories like that at Manchester Bidwell—students who become teachers, who start their own businesses, who get their college degrees and come back to work for us. These are spectacular successes achieved against long odds, but even the less dramatic successes strengthen my faith in the incredible resiliency of the human spirit. In my view, every single mother who lands a job, gets off welfare, and changes the future for her kids; every troubled kid who gets it together and graduates from college; every substance abuser who gets sober and builds a productive life; and every homeless person who gets off the streets is a success story of epic proportions.

Next I called up a slide showing a bright, contemporary classroom. "This is a chem tech class in progress," I said. In the slide, students tapped at logarithmic calculators as they labored to crack the complex mathematical equations written on the board. "These are people who had been saddled with limiting labels: 'welfare mother,' 'drug addict,' 'unemployed,' 'homeless,' 'ex-con,'" I said. "Not one of them had any background in science or math. Yet after a few months they are mastering the skills they need to do complex computations and land jobs as chemical technicians for large local companies like Mylan Labs, Nova Chemicals, and Bayer. Society doesn't expect this kind of thing from people whose potential has been defined and diminished by one restrictive label or another, but when you see accomplishment like this, you can't help but realize how hollow and damaging labels can be."

My next slide showed an image of a sellout crowd filling the seats of an intimate, elegantly proportioned concert hall. "This is our music hall," I said. "We host live jazz concerts here, featuring virtually all the top names in jazz music—artists like Billy Taylor, Dizzy Gillespie, Nancy Wilson, Joe Williams, Dave Brubeck, Milt Jackson, and Chuck Mangione, just to name a few. When I first conceived the idea of adding a jazz component to Manchester Bidwell, I got a lot of puzzled stares. I wasn't surprised. After all, why does a school that teaches arts and job skills need a performance hall? What does jazz have to do with helping our students turn their lives around? At the time, I had no answer for those questions, but jazz music was one of my defining passions, and my heart told me the place wouldn't be complete until jazz was an integral part of its fabric. I never would have predicted that our jazz program would grow to become one of the oldest and most successful jazz subscription series in the country, or that the presence of so much great music, and the relationships we'd build with so many great jazz stars, would lead to the creation of our own jazz label. I certainly never guessed that the albums we produced would win Grammy Awards. But all those things happened, and in the process, jazz has enriched the culture of our school, enhanced our reputation, and earned us new allies and a level of recognition that has opened the doors to unexpected opportunities for growth."

Next up was a shot of the gleaming commercial kitchen that forms the heart of our culinary arts program. "We modeled our food-service curriculum on the Culinary Institute of America," I explained. "The Heinz Corporation contributed most of the equipment and the expertise of some of their executive chefs. Legendary New Orleans chef Paul Prudhomme also helped shape the program. You could pay $30,000 for the same training at a private culinary school. Our students get the training for free," I told them.

"Our graduates are taking good jobs as assistant chefs in fine restaurants all over the city. These are people who came to us thinking a Big Mac was fine dining. But in a matter of months they're turning out dishes like these. . . ." I called up a slide showing a young African-American woman presenting an elegantly garnished platter of trout amandine, followed by a plate of delicate pastries—fruit rolls, miniature scones—each one scalloped, fluted, or otherwise sculpted into a tiny work of art. "This is the kind of work they do after three months of training," I said. "All these are poor people who supposedly have so little to offer, people society has given up on. But if you give them a reason to believe in themselves, if you set the bar high enough and put them in an environment that enables them to perform, you see that they're capable of producing something as fine as these pastries."

The last slide I showed them was another shot of the fountain that flows in the courtyard behind our lobby, and in some ways, this is the most telling slide of all. When we were building the place, I insisted we have a fountain. People thought I was crazy. "Why do you need a fountain in a poverty center?" they asked me. And I told them, "Because this isn't a poverty center, this is a center for success. I want the people who come here to know they deserve success. I start to make that point by letting them know we think they deserve a fountain, and the very fact that a fountain is not, in conventional terms, necessary here makes its presence all the more powerful."

A while ago, some students from our horticultural program took a field trip to visit a large greenhouse in Canada. They spent the day touring the place with the greenhouse managers, discussing techniques and exchanging ideas with the professionals there. On the bus ride home, one of our instructors noticed that one of the students was crying. She was a young mother, an African-American woman, very poor, struggling to raise her kids on welfare. The instructor asked her what was wrong. Fighting off sobs, she said, "They listened to me. I had some good ideas, and they listened. It was the first time anyone treated me like I had something to say. It was the first time around white people that I felt like a human being."

Those were her exact words: She finally felt like *a human being*. All her young life, that woman had been defined by the assumptions society had made about her and by the self-defeating assumptions she was making about herself. That's the real evil of poverty: It diminishes you, it starves you of hope and vision, it forces you to define yourself in terms of what you cannot do or cannot have or cannot be. That insight lies close to the heart of why Manchester Bidwell works, but there is wisdom in it for us all, because once we accept the idea that poverty is, essentially, the acceptance of meager possibility, we can't deny that all of us are in some fashion poor. We all suffer some form of poverty—poverty of imagination, or courage, or vision, or will. We allow ourselves to be limited by our fears—fear of failure, fear of change, fear of being criticized or of looking like a fool. We convince ourselves we lack the resources, the education, or the talent to pursue extraordinary goals. We trust conventional wisdom more than our own intuitions, and we prize the narrow and partial aspects of success— money, power, prestige—more than the rich, whole, satisfyingly human success we imagine in our dreams. In the same fashion that poor folks are shaped and limited by the unforgiving world into which they were born, we all allow ourselves to be defined by the external circumstances of our lives, in terms of what lies beyond our reach, in terms of dreams that will never come true. In the name of "common sense" or "being responsible," we follow the path of least resistance, ignoring our true passions and potential and squandering the chance to live truly extraordinary lives.

For our students at Manchester Bidwell, accepting the notion that dreams can come true often requires heroic levels of courage and faith, but we see that kind of heroism every day: a high school kid on the verge of dropping out turns himself around and goes to college; a welfare mother finds a good-paying job that allows her to build a better future; a homeless woman pulls her life together and buys a decent home. In each of those cases, a human being is finding the strength and the optimism to throw off a lifetime of destructive assumptions and refusing to be limited by false ideas of what is possible and what is not.

Of course, the ghetto has no monopoly on self-defeating assumptions. We all labor under false assumptions that have us living lives that are less than they could be. We all are too easily convinced that we lack the capacity to make our dreams come true. "Impossible" is a frightening word, but my hope, my goal, in writing this book is to help each of you find the valor, the vision, and the conviction to stand up to it and to realize, as so many of our students have, in so many inspiring ways, that you can overcome all the obstacles that stand in your path and live the rich, fulfilling, and meaningfully successful life that all of us, if we are true to our hearts, dream of.

CHAPTER TWO

Growing Up

When I was sixteen years old, I walked up the hill to Oliver High School each morning from our house in Manchester, a poor, low-lying, inner-city neighborhood on the north shore of the Ohio River. I don't remember the sun shining much in Manchester. But I remember looking up sometimes on sunny days and thinking that the broken patches of blue above the shabby row houses of my neighborhood were part of the same blue sky people were seeing in Sewickley and Fox Chapel and other places I'd heard of, places where rich people lived. It wasn't a thought that made me happy or sad; those weren't places I thought about that much, nor were they places I wanted to go. I rarely tried to imagine what it might be like to live in other neighborhoods. I couldn't imagine any place, in fact, besides Manchester and the ghetto that surrounded me. That myopic worldview never worried me when I was young. I simply didn't know any different. But now I know I had fallen for the deadliest lie the ghetto uses to shrink your soul—that *your* world is the *whole* world; that your future, and all the sorry possibilities life will ever offer you, are already right before your eyes.

What I saw as I walked to school each day was an unbroken land-scape of decay that taught me indelible lessons about hopelessness and defeat no matter where my gaze fell. The streets around me were lined with sad, sagging row houses in various states of collapse, their walls made of grimy, mismatched vinyl siding or bowed-out brick. Paint peeled from the rotting window trim. Torn curtains or shredded plastic blinds hung in many of the windows. Some windows had been busted out and repaired with cardboard and tape. Weeds grew wild in vacant lots, as high as my head, and the yards and lots always seemed to be filled with junk—old tires, rusted kitchen appliances, automobile parts, mounds of garbage. We dug things out of the heap to play with, chasing loose trash down the streets. Weeds pushed up through cracks in the asphalt. Graffiti covered the homes, buses, storefronts, abandoned cars, and anything else that stood still long enough, like some colorful insidious vine that claimed everything it touched.

Some of my deepest, most profound memories of childhood are shaded by the ghetto's despair and decay. Sometimes it seemed that every doorknob I touched was blistered with rust. Floorboards groaned under my feet. Stairs creaked and sagged. Many people I knew sat on furniture that was ripped, stained, or worn through to the stuffing. Wallpaper peeled from the walls. Tiles were broken and missing from the linoleum floors. If you could look past the stark reality of it, it was almost cartoonish in appearance: houses leaned this way, porches leaned the other, roofs bowed, walls bulged, doors and windows were wildly out of square. There were some houses that were being maintained in some reasonable fashion—our modest home was one of them—but it's the depressing extent of corruption and decay that dominates my memory of the landscape. In those memories, it sometimes seems I'm gazing at a reflection in some sinister fun-house mirror, warping everything into a parody of what a normal neighborhood should be.

The fact is, I could be describing any of a hundred poor urban neighborhoods across the country. But this was my neighborhood, the place that shaped my outlook on life. It was as if some meanness had infected the neighborhood at its very core and was killing off Manchester from the inside out.

The meanness that pervaded Manchester affected the people who lived there, too. I passed ruined people in my neighborhood every morning on my way to school. Some of them scared me—the scam artists, the drug dealers, the predators and small-time hoods. You had to give them a wide berth or they'd find a way to get a piece of your life. Others simply saddened me: people who were lost, frightened, hollow, and used up. Somewhere along the line their lives had jumped the track. I'd see junkies make a buy, then slip into an alley to shoot up while we junior high school kids walked around them. I'd see men I knew, grown men with wives and families, hanging on corners, acting the fool, smoking dope or passing a bottle in a brown paper bag at eight o'clock in the morning. Hookers would say hello to me, make lewd comments, and laugh. I knew some of them, knew their pimps.

Those were the broken people, the ones who had lost the will, or the strength, to fight the lure of the streets. Most folks in Manchester tried to fight, heroically sometimes, with whatever resources they could muster. But the undertow was relentless and sometimes even the best got sucked down. Say a kid does his best to stay out of trouble, works hard at school, keeps clear of bad places, avoids the wrong crowd. One day he's walking home. It's cold. He's tired. A car pulls over. The driver is a teenager he knew when he was a kid. *How you doing?* the driver asks. *Haven't seen you in a while. Lemme give you a ride.* The driver doesn't mention that the car is stolen. When the cops pull them over a little while later, both boys get booked. Just like that, that kid isn't a good kid anymore. He has a record. If he's old enough, he'll do time. Whatever future he dreamed of has just been stolen away.

It's just that easy to fall through one of the ghetto's trapdoors. It takes only one small lapse in judgment. Being in the wrong place at the wrong time—and there are so many wrong places and wrong times. I knew a guy named Ronnie in Manchester; he and I grew up together. Ronnie was always a stand-up guy. Smart. Funny. Interesting. Loyal. He was a responsible guy, never caused trouble, never found himself on the wrong side of the law. But one day Ronnie walked into a Manchester tavern, confronted a patron at the bar, pulled out a revolver, and shot the guy through the head, killing him. Then he took a seat at the bar and waited for the cops to come.

Ronnie served less than seven years in prison for his crime, and one day, after his release, I ran into him on the street. He met me with his usual hearty greeting. "What are you up to, man?" he asked me. "How's your brother? How's your mom?" We talked like nothing had changed, as if he hadn't walked into that bar that day and taken some man's life. When the conversation lulled, I asked the question I had to know the answer to: "Ronnie, why'd you do it, man?"

Ronnie nodded soberly. "I heard he was after my girlfriend, man," he said. "You know I don't put up with that."

There was no trace of macho bluster in his voice when he said this. His demeanor was calm, almost modest, as if I would recognize the position he'd been in and understand that he had had no other choice.

It was simple for Ronnie: He had been disrespected. He had taken care of business. He had shown himself to be a man.

Now, here's the thing about Ronnie: If I ran into him today, I'd be happy to see him. I'd have things to tell him. We'd share some laughs. We'd have the same good chemistry we'd always had. And I'd have to face a sobering truth: Ronnie and I are not so different. We have a common past. Our characters, our interests, and our ways of looking at the world were similar enough for us to be friends. But for some reason, on one particular day, Ronnie decided that his best course of action was to blow some guy's head off, even if it meant he'd go to prison. I hold Ronnie responsible for his actions. Poverty is no excuse for doing crime. But I know his world. I know how it distorts your vision, sucks the hope from your soul. I know how it cheapens life, hardens hearts, and warps human emotions. There are lots of Ronnies in Manchester, guys I grew up with who got tripped up, dragged down, strung out, or otherwise defeated by a life devoid of hope. Hope is the one thing, the only thing that inoculates you from the madness, wherever you live. But where on those mean streets does a person find hope?

MANCHESTER WASN'T ALWAYS such a broken place. When I was a toddler it was a stable, integrated, working-class community where African-American families lived side by side with the descendants of Greek, Italian, Middle Eastern, and Eastern European immigrants who had flocked to Pittsburgh at the turn of the nineteenth century for jobs in the region's sprawling factories and mills. The streets were lined with modest but well-maintained houses. People tended flower beds and vegetable gardens. The nearby churches were anchors for the entire neighborhood, and we all turned out, regardless of denomination or ethnic heritage, for the celebrations that marked the various festivals and feast days. Sometimes there were formal processions, with banners, marching bands, and statues of saints being carried through the streets. Often there were street fairs, open to all. The mixed ethnic flavor of the neighborhood attracted me. You could walk down a single block and smell the spices and aromas of cuisines from all over the world: the rich smell of tomato sauce cooking in the Italian households, moussaka baking in the ovens of the Greeks, the smell of butter and onions with which the Eastern Europeans prepared their pierogies. It *was* a place where people worked hard, took care of their homes, tried to make a better life for themselves and their families, and did their best to get along. The kind of place where a kid could go anywhere he wanted and never feel unwelcome or afraid.

That Manchester began to crumble in the mid-1960s. The first blow came when the Allis-Chalmers Corporation, which manufactured industrial equipment, closed its huge plant on Pittsburgh's North Side and a lot of Manchester wage earners lost their jobs. Many of these workers, most of them white, moved their families out of the neighborhood in search of jobs in other places, draining away much of the neighborhood's working-class vitality, leaving vacancies that caused property values to rapidly decline.

Then, a few years later, the Pennsylvania Department of Transportation began construction on a new highway bypass connecting downtown Pittsburgh with Ohio River Boulevard, a busy commuter artery that led from the city to the northern suburbs lining the banks of the Ohio. Before the bypass, commuters had to travel on surface streets through Manchester to and from work. But the new highway bypassed Manchester, literally rising above it—it was an elevated road, built on massive concrete pylons, so that drivers barely got a glimpse of a Manchester rooftop or two as they sped by.

The new road simplified life for the commuters, but it was a devastating blow for the people who now lived in its shadow. By rerouting traffic to bypass the streets of Manchester, planners had turned the neighborhood into an instant backwater. Businesses withered. The community was physically cut off from the lifeblood of the city. It was as if an entire city neighborhood had suddenly dropped into the shadows and become invisible. (Even today, many Pittsburghers don't know where Manchester is, even though they pass over it every day.)

The neighborhood also suffered from the physical imposition of the highway. To make a path for the bypass and the maze of access ramps that serve it, builders leveled whole city blocks through the residential heart of the neighborhood, bisecting the community into two severed halves. Land that was once the site of homes, churches, shops, and playgrounds was now a lifeless concrete corridor, dominated by the massive piers that formed the highway's foundation and the massive retaining walls that rose like the barricades of a fortress.

The bypass snuffed out whatever vitality was left in Manchester, and the neighborhood rapidly declined. Property values bottomed out. Anyone who could afford it fled the neighborhood, leaving a void that was filled by poor blacks from other parts of the city looking for cheaper places to live. Most of these people had lived in abject poverty for generations. When they arrived they brought with them all the complex problems that poverty breeds: drugs, crime, desperation, despair. As the years passed and no one on the outside noticed or took action, these problems festered and deepened, turning Manchester into a ghetto. By the time I was entering high school, I barely remembered the old Manchester at all.

MOST OF US are not called on to perform heroic acts as a part of our daily routines. In the ghetto, however, the simplest actions—holding on to hope in the face of hopelessness, for example—can take on heroic dimensions.

No one fought that battle more vigilantly than my mother, Evelyn. I never saw my mother surrender a single inch to the ghetto. She fought with all her considerable strength and energy to keep the coarseness and dangers of the streets at bay, and to create an atmosphere of safety and sanity in our home so that my younger brother, Mark, and I could have some semblance of a normal childhood.

My mother took great care to always be carefully coiffed and groomed. She carried herself with poise and dignity wherever she went, and she spoke with perfect diction, despite the neighbors' whispered complaints that she was putting on airs. She was never deterred by those whispers.

"Just because we're poor," she'd say, "we don't have to live like defeated people."

She taught us how to present ourselves to the world, hounding us on our personal hygiene, always checking that our fingernails were clean, that our hair was neatly trimmed and combed, and that our clothes were freshly laundered. She taught us manners and demanded that we treat her, and others, with respect. While our tiny row house was a humble home, she made it a place we would all take pride in.

"I don't care what's going on outside that door," she would tell us. "In here we live by my rules. And rule number one is, this place is going to be *clean*." And she made sure that my brother and I were part of the cleanup crew, making the beds, keeping our clothes in order, picking up after ourselves. Saturday mornings we had to scrub the floors. She taught us that there was a right way and a wrong way to scrub floors, and that we would be doing it the right way—that is, *her* way. We began in the kitchen with buckets of clean hot water, lots of Ajax, scrub brushes, fresh cotton rags. My mother believed that the only way to get a floor really clean was to get up close and personal with it, so she made my brother and me get on our knees. First we scrubbed with the stiff brushes to get the dirt out from the cracks and crevices between the boards. Then we changed the water, scrubbed some more, changed the water again, and washed the floor with the rags before rinsing away the dirt. We kept at it as long as it took until my mother pronounced it clean. Then we repeated the process throughout the house—bedrooms, bathroom, living room—and when all the wood was clean and dry, we'd get down on our knees to coat the floors with paste wax and polish them until they gleamed.

I hated that job intensely—it took hours. But to this day I remember how those shining floors transformed the way it felt to live in that old house, giving us a sense of pride in its fresh and gleaming appearance. Still, the bigger satisfaction was the smile on my mother's face when we were through. I knew her smile was about more than a shiny floor. She was celebrating another small victory against the entropy and moral disorder of the streets just outside our door.

The streets were not my mother's only source of struggle. She also had to deal with my father, who, for most of my childhood, brought the street life my mother was trying so hard to fend off into the heart of our home. William Strickland Senior was a smart man, resourceful and talented, who had the potential to make something worthwhile of his life. As a sergeant in the Army, he oversaw the care and feeding of thousands of soldiers a day. After his discharge from the service, he became a highly skilled plasterer and finish carpenter specializing in fine cabinetwork, intricate wood molding, and the repair and restoration of ornate plaster in old Pittsburgh homes. Sometimes, when I was young, he would take me to a job site and show off the work he was doing. This was my father at his best, confident, proud, and I liked that he shared that with me. I'm not sure when my father's life began to unravel, but by the time I was twelve or thirteen years old he was a man of the streets in the streets. He gambled. He drank. Sometimes he'd disappear for days at a time, leaving my mother home alone with bills to pay and an empty refrigerator. My mother's impulse was to shield us as best she could from this hard reality and preserve the illusion, at least, of a stable family. But there were times when her patience ran thin.

I remember one Christmas morning when I was around fourteen years old. My mother's spirits were always high during the holidays. She loved everything about Christmas and wanted it to be a special time for us, too. She had decorated the house, baked cookies, and brought home a tree, which we trimmed together. Somehow, she found money to buy presents for both of us, and on Christmas Day, she promised us a feast.

She had already started cooking when my brother and I came down on Christmas morning. I saw my father in the doorway, wearing his coat.

"Where are you going?" she asked.

"I'll be back in an hour," he answered.

"It's Christmas," my mother complained. Then I saw my father walking out the door.

My mother said nothing about my father to me. She steered me to the tree and I tore into my presents. But I could feel the tension in the air.

Hours later, there was no sign of my father. My mother worked furiously at the stove, her glance constantly shifting from the clock to the door. Around four o'clock, dinner was ready. My mother, with grim determination, looked at me and said, "Go find him." She was determined that her sons would have Christmas dinner with their father.

I looked for him at the Hi-Hat, a local bar, then at Chappies, but he was nowhere to be found. Finally, I checked Mr. Felix's barbershop. Mr. Felix cut hair in the front of his shop, but in the back he ran a poolroom and a bar. I found my father in the back, passed out on the pool table.

"Come on, Dad," I said, "dinner's ready."

He grumbled and tried to swat me away, but I kept after him and finally got him to his feet and led him home. He slumped into his seat at the dinner table, surly, silent, reeking of booze. But we had our Christmas dinner. It was not the happiest day, but I had long since stopped expecting my father to bring us happiness. What hurt me the most was the fear I saw in my little brother's eyes and the pain it caused my mother. She tried so hard to show us what a good life might feel like. She set an example with her dignity and strength. She wanted to instill in us confidence and hope. But sometimes she couldn't meet the challenge. Even as a kid I saw the worry lines around her eyes, the way she shivered every time she heard about another life being claimed by the streets, and the tears she tried to hide when we'd come home from the grocery store and she'd have to chase the junkies off the stoop so we could get into our house.

My mother believed that education was the ticket to a better life, so she did everything she could to make sure my brother and I took our studies seriously. Out of respect for her, I pretended to work hard. But the fact was, I had no heart for school. When I walked up the hill each morning toward Oliver High, I knew what was waiting for me at the top: another day of burned-out teachers rambling on about the gross national product or the square root of some ridiculously large number. Another day of mind-numbing boredom on subjects that had nothing to do with the world I lived in. My mother hoped education would show me my future, but I couldn't even imagine a future. Or maybe I just couldn't bear the thought of any future I *could* imagine. So I showed up at school each day, put my time in, coasted, cut classes, did only what was necessary to scrape by. By the time I was beginning my senior year, I just wanted school to end, even though I had no idea of what I'd do after graduation.

One morning, as I was ambling unhappily along the hallway toward my homeroom, I caught the smell of fresh coffee. I followed it to the door of the art room and looked inside. It was a sunny morning and light was streaming in through the big double-hung windows. Jazz was playing in the background—at least I thought it was jazz. The light and the rich smell of the coffee drew me into the room.

At the rear of the room I saw someone sitting with his back to me, a white guy of average build, with a short dark beard and longish hair.

He was dressed stylishly for the era in a leather vest, striped shirt, corduroy trousers, and desert boots. His head was bowed forward, his elbows tight against his sides. He was rocking gently on his stool. What caught my eye was the way he was moving his hands. He held them in front of him at waist level and was moving them, slowly and mysteriously, up and down, like a hypnotist or a sorcerer conjuring a spell.

I got closer and looked over his shoulder. He was leaning over some kind of turntable. On the table was a ball of something gray and wet. His hands were on that glistening ball, coaxing it, shaping it, and as he worked the ball it seemed to come magically alive. It sprang up to form a cylinder, then the lower half of the cylinder swelled gracefully into the shape of a bell. He shifted his hands and now the top edge of the cylinder curled to form a thin, graceful lip. He worked this way for a while, patiently, carefully, then he moved his hands away and I saw a small, perfect vase spinning on the table. I couldn't have been more amazed if the guy had caused the vase to appear by simply snapping his fingers. I had a hundred questions, but before I could open my mouth the man at the wheel looked up from his work.

"Mr. Strickland," he said jovially. "How have you been?"

I was startled to recognize Frank Ross, an art teacher I'd known in my sophomore year. I remembered Mr. Ross as a very hip dude who had a passion for art and teaching, and a reputation for treating his students like human beings instead of a bunch of unteachable deadheads. I'd had him for a photography class in tenth grade—one of the few classes I'd ever looked forward to—but he went on sabbatical during my junior year and I assumed he was gone for good.

Frank asked me about my summer, about the classes I was taking, and I mumbled some responses. But my thoughts were scattered. I couldn't get my mind off the magic Frank had just worked with the clay. I watched as Frank turned off the potter's wheel, then used a thin strand of wire, stretched tight in his hands, to carefully cut the pot free from the surface of the wheel. Then he used something that looked like a spatula to lift the pot from the turntable and place it on a nearby wooden rack.

"What happens next?" I asked.

"I'll let it dry for a while," Frank answered. "Then I'll put it back on the wheel and trim off all the rough spots before it gets too hard."

"How do you get it to look like this?" I was pointing at a small bowl with a smooth, gleaming finish, glowing with rich tones of brown, black, and red.

"That one is finished," he said. "It's been glazed and fired in the kiln."

I had no idea what those words meant, but they made my heart pound. Frank saw the look on my face and smiled.

"You want to try it?" he asked.

He didn't have to ask me twice. I set my books on a counter and slipped onto the stool where Frank had been sitting. Frank loaded some clay on the wheel.

"Keep your elbows against your sides and use your body to keep your hands steady," he said. Then he showed me how to hold my hands to shape the clay. "Use the base of your thumb and your little finger," he said. "Press firmly, but be gentle. And don't get your hopes up. Getting a pot to stand up on the wheel is a difficult task, as hard as hitting a big-league curveball. You have to get the feel for it, and that only comes from trying."

I nodded and Frank turned on the wheel. I saw right away that he was right, the clay was impossible to manage. Under my clumsy touch it bulged and swelled into comical shapes, wobbled, leaned, tottered, and finally flopped onto its side. But I didn't care. I knew the moment I started that there was magic in the clay. It was the way it felt in my hands, so clean, smooth, simple, whole, and alive. Nothing I'd ever touched felt like that—like raw potential, like *possibility.* Looking back, I know that something in the feel of the clay was feeding a deep hunger in my soul. But I wasn't thinking that way then; I was only caught up in the thrill of the experience. I didn't want that feeling to end.

Frank let me work for a while, smiling as I turned out one laughable failure after another, then finally he pulled the plug. "You should get to homeroom," he told me. "But if you're interested in this stuff, sign up for my class. It's not too late to get you in."

I did sign up for Frank's class, and Frank's classroom quickly became the epicenter of my senior year. I was never late for Frank's class, and I never wanted to leave when it was over. There was something powerful in the space that Frank had created. The light, the jazz, the smell of the constantly brewing coffee, the quiet sense of industry he fostered, even the orderliness and care with which he insisted we clean and store our tools and supplies—all these things added up to an atmosphere of purpose, calmness, and sanity, something I couldn't find in the streets where I lived. I knew in my gut that room was a place that could heal a lot of old deep wounds, and I wanted to spend as much time in that place as possible.

We worked hard in Frank's class, and as the weeks passed and I logged more time at the wheel, I started to get a feel for the clay. I finished some basic pieces—cups, plates, simple bowls—and each of these small successes fed the feeling I had the first time I laid my hands on clay: that I was nourishing something basic in my spirit, that I was holding sheer potential in my hands. For the first time in my life, I found myself believing that something extraordinary was within my grasp. I didn't know at the time that my passion for clay would set me on a path to a new future; I was still too much a child of the ghetto to think that way. I really wasn't thinking about the future at all. I was only thinking about the wonderful way clay made me *feel*. I'd been living in a chronic state of depression, but until I discovered clay, I never really noticed the sadness that weighed on my heart any more than a fish notices water. I didn't know that my spirit was slowly dying. The joy of working with clay showed me what it was like to feel truly alive, and I wanted to sustain that feeling. I wanted to push back the darkness a little and make some room for my spirit to breathe. I had no larger vision than that. I only wanted to feel better, to improve the quality of my existence *then and there*.

As weeks passed, my beginner's passion for working with clay matured into a more serious sense of discipline and commitment. I became a true student of the art form, reading the books Frank suggested, visualizing the pieces I'd like to make, and spending lots of time at the wheel, honing my skills and techniques. The quality of my work improved dramatically. Unfortunately, my success in Mr. Ross's class didn't extend to my other subjects—with the exception of an English class taught by another influential teacher of mine, Mr. Dick Verschell. Mr. Verschell had the same ability as Mr. Ross to make his subject matter come alive for me. He didn't care about where I lived or what other teachers might expect from me; he taught me how to read Shakespeare as if he had no doubt it would have relevance and meaning in my life, and thanks to his brilliance as a teacher, it did. I always gave him my best effort, and he recognized my work with As. But otherwise, I was cutting classes more than ever and hiding out in the art room, working on pots. When my grades started sliding and my teachers began to grumble, Mr. Ross spoke on my behalf.

"This kid's on fire," he told them, "and I think he has potential. Can't you cut him some slack?"

To my amazement, all my teachers went along. As long as I met their minimal requirements, they passed me with Cs and looked the other way when I cut their classes. Being no fool, I showed my appreciation by offering them the prettiest pots I made.

THROWING POTS is a maddeningly difficult and unpredictable process.

The first challenge is to center the clay on the wheel, an apparently straightforward task that, in fact, requires an almost Zen-like sense of patience and deftness. If you're off by a centimeter, you may as well be off by a mile. A lump of clay that is not perfectly centered is doomed from the start. No matter how carefully you try to shape it, it will only fall in on itself as the potter's wheel spins, or simply whirl itself to pieces. You learn to center clay through sheer repetition, by trying and failing again and again, until finally you get the feel. But centering clay is only the first hurdle. Next you must shape the clay into something worth making. This requires an artistic eye, but you must also find the perfect balance between force and forgiveness in order to give the piece a pleasing and symmetrical profile. Use too light a touch and centrifugal force might cause the piece to bloat and sag.

Too firm a hand could crush it. This balance is devilishly difficult to achieve, and it changes according to the size, shape, and complexity of the piece you're creating, and also with the thickness of the clay.

It's a skill that does not come easily, but once you master it you can count on turning out a halfway decent pot almost every time you try. But that's just the start of the process. When you've finished throwing the piece—that is, when you're happy with the shape you've created at the wheel—it must be set aside to dry. This takes about a week. Then the piece goes back to the wheel so that any burrs, rough patches, and edges can be trimmed. After that, it's back to the drying rack for a few more days. Then the piece can be fired in the kiln, where heat transforms the clay into ceramic. After cooling and a few more days of rest, a glaze is applied and the piece goes into the kiln for its final firing. Finally, you open the kiln and lift out a finished work of art—if you've done everything right, that is, and if luck is on your side. The truth is, there are a thousand ways for the process to go wrong. Maybe you worked the piece too thin. Or you got a batch of bad clay. Your glaze could fail or the humidity might have been wrong for proper drying. Sometimes, you do everything right and it's still not enough—you open the kiln and find your piece in shards.

Working with clay is an enterprise that's riddled with uncertainty and unfairness, and the failures can break your heart. But once in a while you reach into that kiln and pull out a piece of work that is everything you'd hoped for. Those moments were what I lived for. They gave me a high that was better than anything the streets could offer—the same rush of joy and amazement you feel when a prayer is answered or a dream comes true—and they showed me that working with clay was really all about dreaming and having the courage to hope. There are so many disappointments along the way, but then one day, out of mud and imagination, you create something lovely and worthwhile, and it feels like nothing less than a miracle. That's what Frank Ross taught me: Miracles happen. You can mold them with your hands.

BY THE MIDDLE of my senior year, I was a completely different person from the one I'd been when I first walked into Frank Ross's room: I was focused, disciplined, optimistic, and more mature. Mr. Ross seemed pleased with these developments and with the progress I was making with my pots.

"You're getting pretty good at this," he told me one day, examining a big dinner platter I had just taken out of the kiln. "Good enough for a show, maybe." He encouraged me to approach some local galleries and ask them to exhibit some of my stuff. I did, and to my amazement, one of them said yes. A date was set for a small show. And just like that I became an exhibiting artist. I dressed up for my opening night, invited a bunch of neighborhood folks, shook hands as people came in, and answered questions about my work. The smile on my mother's face was priceless. I even sold a piece or two.

"Congratulations," Mr. Ross said, and he chuckled when I showed him the modest checks my patrons had written out for me. "You're a professional artist now."

At Mr. Ross's urging, I started to enter some pieces in juried shows around the city. More often than not, my work was accepted. Sometimes, I won awards. One piece I made won a Gold Key Award for outstanding work by a student from the Pittsburgh schools. More astonishingly, thanks to the web of contacts Frank helped me to establish in the local art world, I was asked to appear as a demonstrating artist at the Three Rivers Arts Festival, Pittsburgh's largest public celebration of the arts.

The annual festival brings in big-name artists from all over the world and draws crowds in the thousands to open-air galleries set up in the parks and on the sidewalks of the city's downtown area. Festival organizers set me up at a demonstration booth near Point State Park with a potter's wheel and some bags of clay, and told me to get started. Soon a crowd had gathered around to watch. People started asking questions. They were pointing me out to their kids, smiling in appreciation of what I was doing, applauding when I finished! It was a revelation. These folks, most of them white, saw past all the labels they might have otherwise used to define me: *Disadvantaged. Black. Poor.* They were seeing me as a person, with something unique to offer. They were defining me in terms of my talent and skill. They were seeing me as an *artist.* Man, the way that felt helped to turn my whole world around.

More important, of course, was the fact that I was developing a new way of seeing myself. It literally reshaped the way I saw my place in the world. My family still had no money. My father was still AWOL most of the time. And I still had to face the insanity that swirled around me on the Manchester streets. I wasn't naive enough to think my modest success with clay would put an end to all my problems. I expected my life to be difficult and filled with struggle, as always. But I had reason to struggle now, and that made all the difference. I sensed a sea change in my life. It was as if a terrible storm had passed and daylight was breaking through the clouds. The air seemed fresh, clean, and new. My senses seemed keener, colors seemed brighter, I felt a lightness of spirit I'd never known before. It was the simple joy of being alive, and it gave me a whole new perspective on who I was. That is the power of hope, and it's not just poor folks who need to grasp that insight. Every one of us needs something to hope for, to change the biography of our lives. For so long I had allowed myself to be defined by circumstances of the world around me. I accepted all the labels, the limitations placed upon me, the low expectations others had for me. I let myself believe that the only opportunities available to me were the ones the streets of Manchester would allow. But now I had a new basis for my self-identity, anchored in my skill, passion, talent, and achievement, things that Manchester couldn't cheapen or corrupt, things that were irreversibly, undeniably *mine*.

I was finished with defining myself in terms of what I didn't have and what I couldn't be. Instead, I focused on what I had inside me and who I already was. I realized that a meaningful life was not some abstract thing drifting off in an unattainable future. Life was right *now*, and even if I never got out of Manchester, I already had at my fingertips everything I needed to build a rich and meaningful life. Some of the richest people I ever met have yet to realize this. And as a result, they remain poor in spirit. That insight changed everything for me. I still didn't have any money, but I didn't think like a poor kid anymore.

I GRADUATED FROM Oliver High School by the skin of my teeth in 1967. With Frank's intercession—and despite my lackluster grades and anemic SATs—I was accepted at the University of Pittsburgh on a probationary basis, becoming one of only a few black students in Pitt's huge freshman class. Pitt's admissions people didn't think I had a strong enough background in art to enroll in their arts department, so I majored in history instead. I hoped to become a teacher someday and maybe help some kids the way that Frank had helped me. I kept working on my clay, building my skills, and solidifying my modest profile in the arts community. Frank had now become a trusted friend. He welcomed me into his home almost as part of his family, and made me part of the ever-present circle of artists, musicians, professors, and other creative individuals who gathered there. Over long, elaborate dinners in Frank's big dining room, I shared in conversations about art, jazz, politics, travel, philosophy, and good food. I learned a lot from the people I met there; I liked the way they listened when I talked, as if they were truly interested in what I had to say. Frank's house quickly became a sanctuary for me, just as his classroom had been at school. Sometimes when I was sitting there, listening to the jazz that was always playing in the background, savoring the vitality and life that was always present in that house, I couldn't believe my good fortune. I was now a college boy, a rising artist, with lots of creative work at hand and a circle of hip, supportive friends. When I drove home from Frank's house to Manchester, that sense of good fortune traveled with me. My life was swinging, man. Manchester didn't seem so big and bad anymore. I was beginning to think that I had broken the hold the neighborhood had on me. A good life was possible. A bright future seemed to grow brighter every day.

But then, in the spring of 1968, a bullet fired in Memphis seemed to set the world on fire, and showed me that Manchester wouldn't give up its grip on me so easily.

CHAPTER THREE

A Dream Is Born

On April 4, 1968, Martin Luther King was shot and killed in Memphis while appearing on a balcony of the Lorraine Motel. That evening, I sat in heartbroken silence in the living room of our house as a shaken Walter Cronkite made the announcement on the evening news. At first, I refused to accept it. *This great man can't be gone,* I thought. When the full reality of Dr. King's death seized me, my outrage and grief wouldn't let me sit still, and I found myself out in the streets, wandering aimlessly through the neighborhood. There were people everywhere, gathered on stoops and street corners. Some were weeping or simply staring in disbelief. In the distance I heard angry voices and the sounds of commotion. I headed in the direction of the noise, and when I rounded the corner of one street, I saw an eerie scene. A car was sitting motionless in the middle of the intersection. There were two white guys inside. A small crowd of young men from the neighborhood had them surrounded. It took me a long moment to believe what I was seeing—the men were pelting the car with rocks. They had already shattered the car's side windows. Then one of them stepped in front of the car. I recognized the guy as a bad actor from the neighborhood. As I watched in disbelief, he threw a brick through the car's windshield. The shattering of the windshield glass seemed to rouse the dazed driver, who gathered his wits and gunned the engine. His tires jumped the curb as he swung the car around, and the crowd chucked more rocks after him as he sped away. My heart sank as I saw that. I understood the rage, and I can't say I didn't feel like smashing something myself. But there was trouble in the air that night, and I knew no good could come of this kind of violence.

What I didn't know was that violence was erupting in other parts of Manchester and around the country as well. Shots had been fired, fires had been set, and angry crowds were gathering. The Pittsburgh police had already dispatched a battalion of cops in riot gear to the neighborhood in hopes of keeping order. But the heavy police presence only inflamed the tension, and in the days and weeks that followed, Manchester, like other black neighborhoods across America, became a combat zone. Protest demonstrations turned ugly as demonstrators, in defiance of everything Dr. King stood for, smashed storefront windows, looted shops, and set cars and buildings on fire. The cops fought back with tear gas, guard dogs, and billy clubs. When the police failed to establish order, National Guard troops were called in to patrol the streets. Sharpshooters were stationed on rooftops and curfews were established. A chapter of the national Black Panther Party took up residence in Manchester to add its militant voice to the angry fray. The toll of the riots was heavy: Businesses were destroyed, homes were ruined, and lives were lost. The first casualty came when an older white man—a longtime Manchester resident—spotted an eight-year-old African-American boy trespassing in his garden and shot him with a deer rifle from his bedroom window. I saw another of the casualties firsthand. I was walking in the neighborhood when I saw a squad car parked in the street. Nearby, some people were standing over the body of a young boy, fourteen years old or so, lying dead beside the curb. They told me the kid had stolen a radio, or some foolish thing, from a looted store. A cop saw him running and ordered him to stop, but the kid kept running. The policeman shot him in the back of the head. It's impossible to describe the emotional desolation I felt as I stood there watching that fallen boy. It was like the mouth of hell had opened up and let me look in. Madness was loose in the neighborhood. It felt like the world was pulling itself apart at the seams.

The riots raged on and off all that summer, casting a dark shadow over my life at the very time I was taking my first real strides toward a brighter future. I had started classes at the University of Pittsburgh that fall, one of only a handful of black students in a freshman class that numbered in the thousands, and one of only two in the Department of History, the subject I'd selected as my major. Immersed, for the first time, in a world of white experience and values, I found it hard to find my bearings. Most of the white kids in my classes had grown up in stable neighborhoods and had graduated from good schools. They came to Pitt with a natural confidence and expectations of high achievement, and it was clear to me from the very start that they had been prepared, in ways that were beyond me, to make their dreams come true. I saw it in their eyes as we sat through our first lectures. They were connecting with the professors—grasping concepts and arguments—in ways I couldn't fathom. Their questions were pertinent and informed. They seemed to be tapping into a web of insight and understanding that I simply wasn't part of.

It amazed me, for example, that they would all dip their heads in unison to jot down notes when the professor made some apparently important comment. What were they hearing? For me, the same lecture was an indecipherable landslide of random facts, opaque concepts, and elusive theories. I lacked the learning skills I needed to manage that flood of information. I didn't know how to connect all those dots. Lacking the practiced ear of my classmates, I compensated by writing down, verbatim, everything the professor said, hoping I could figure it all out later. It was a disastrous strategy, of course; as I frantically scribbled my way through my classes, I completely missed the meaning of the points my professors were trying to convey. Later, when I tried to make sense of those notes, I found that whatever wisdom they might contain was lost in the verbal sprawl that filled the pages. Studying them only left me more confused, and my confusion filled me with self-doubt. Was I kidding myself that I could make it in the white world? I knew I was smart, and I was willing to work as hard as anyone to succeed. But the kids I was competing with seemed to be following a set of rules I'd never heard of. I was simply not prepared for the complexity of the course content I was facing, or for the velocity at which we moved through the material. No one had ever expected me to learn so much so fast. I didn't have the base of knowledge or the study skills I needed to keep my head above water. My first weeks of college left me reeling, and as I struggled to find my balance, I knew my future hung in the balance. I had been accepted at Pitt as a probationary student, and by the terms of my probation, I needed to maintain a C average across all my classes or I'd be booted out of school. As the semester progressed and I continued to struggle, I knew that if I made the grade that term, I would do it by the skin of my teeth. So I struggled through my homework in my bedroom each night, as sirens wailed in the streets and angry crowds gathered, reminding me of the world I came from and making me wonder if I was a fool to think I could survive in any other.

AS MEAGER AS my college-level study skills may have been, I knew enough about basic math and science to help younger kids in my community, so, in the summer after high school, I started tutoring grade school kids at a neighborhood center in Manchester. Frank Ross had shown me what a noble profession teaching could be, and it was my plan to teach history if I survived at Pitt long enough to earn my degree. Helping my students do better in school felt right to me, and I liked the idea that maybe I was giving them some small measure of what Mr. Ross had given me. My work at the center also introduced me to a new group of good people, activists and community organizers who were giving their time to make Manchester a better place. One of them was a young Episcopalian minister named Tom Cox. Tom was part of an organization called North Side Christian Ministry, a group of urban ministers, most of them white guys, trying to do some good in places like Manchester. Tom knew about my art and my struggles at Pitt, and he knew the emotional toll the riots had taken on my spirits. He knew how much I hated the racism and the heavy-handed presence of the cops, but he knew I was troubled by the self-destructive actions of my neighbors, too.

"I can't stand this," I told him. "It's weighing on me, man, like I can't find space to live my life. And there's nothing I can do."

"Maybe there is," Tom replied. "The church has some money available for community-improvement projects in the neighborhood. We're looking for people who want to improve things. If you have any ideas, let me know. Think about what you have to offer."

What do I have to offer? I asked myself. To my surprise, the answer came quickly: I had my passion for clay. I thought of the kids I saw at the neighborhood center. These were kids who had endured the ghetto's dehumanizing abuses since they were born. Now they had to face the madness going on in the streets every day, and their eyes were clouded with worry. Would working with clay do for them what it did for me? Could I create for them the same kind of safe, nurturing space I'd found in Mr. Ross's classroom? I pictured the kids in a bright, clean pottery studio, a safe, orderly place where they could escape, for a while at least, the fears that weighed them down. But I wasn't thinking just about the kids. When I envisioned that space in my mind, I knew it was something I needed as much as they did.

"Maybe I could start an arts center," I said to Tom. "Teach kids to work with clay."

Tom smiled thoughtfully. "Put a proposal together," he said. "I'll take it to the bishop."

A few weeks later, I handed Tom a proposal for a small community arts center that would serve the children of Manchester—essentially, an operation that would expose kids to the same transforming experiences Mr. Ross's art classes had provided for me. Tom liked the proposal, and a few days later he took me to meet Robert Appleyard, bishop of the Episcopalian diocese of Pittsburgh. The bishop liked the proposal enough to put us in touch with potential funders. "I want you to go see Toby Biddle," he said. "He's head of the vestry at St. Michael's Parish in Ligonier. I've already told him about you, and he's interested in working with you, if you can convince them you can pull this off."

We scheduled a meeting at St. Michael's. On the appointed day, Tom picked me up in his bright green Porsche at my mother's house in Manchester.

"Ever been to Ligonier before?" Tom asked as we drove out of the neighborhood.

"Not in this lifetime," I said, and laughed. Ligonier, which lay about an hour and a half southeast of Pittsburgh, in the rural Laurel Mountains of Westmoreland County, had been settled as a frontier outpost in colonial times and was the site of some key skirmishes in the French and Indian War. But it wasn't an outpost anymore. Now the rolling hills surrounding the town were home to pristine horse farms, exclusive country clubs, steeplechase races, and the country estates of powerful Pittsburgh industrialists. It was a perfect fall day as we raced in Tom's Porsche on the two-lane blacktop highway that wound through the mountains toward Ligonier, and the wooded mountains blazed in full autumn colors. We passed grand houses and horses trotting in rolling green pastures lined with long whitewashed fences. The sky was an electric blue and the air was filled with the fragrance of wild laurel, from which the mountains get their name. Just when I thought the countryside couldn't get any more picturesque, we rounded a curve and I spotted figures on horseback riding on the berm: two women, decked out in red blazers, black helmets, knee boots, and jodhpurs, with a brace of hounds trailing the horses.

"Foxhunt," said Tom, as he spotted the puzzlement in my eyes. Before I could say anything, we heard the wail of a siren behind us and a state cop pulled us over.

"Were we speeding, officer?" Tom asked.

The trooper bent down and looked me over. "Where are you gentlemen from?" he asked.

"Pittsburgh," Tom answered. "We're on our way to St. Michael's church. We have an appointment with Reverend Smith."

The trooper nodded. He took a look at Tom's Porsche, took another look at me, and asked us to wait while he returned to the squad car. Moments later, he returned. He thanked us for our time, urged us to drive safely, and sent us on our way.

When we were back on the road, Tom shot me a sly smile and muttered, "Welcome to Ligonier . . ."

Moments later, we arrived at St. Michael's. I was expecting something grand and imposing. What I saw, instead, was a simple country chapel, straight out of Currier & Ives, clad in crisply painted white clapboards, with a graceful steeple pointing up toward the blue mountain sky. Reverend Max Smith met us as we parked the car. Toby Biddle, president of St. Michael's vestry, was with him, and together we toured the church's Colonial interior, which hadn't been altered since the chapel was built in the 1800s. Then we drove to Reverend Smith's home, where we met the rest of the vestry—the people who would hear my plea for funding. Max's house was a large, tastefully furnished stone cottage drenched in sunlight and decorated in a relaxed but quietly elegant English country style. The members of the vestry were gathered out back in the garden. We joined them, and Tom introduced me. An attractive woman in a sundress caught my eye.

"Tall or short?" she asked.

Confused, I looked to Tom for some help. He lifted his glass to tip me off; she was offering me a cocktail.

"Short," I said, wondering what made her think I would understand cocktail party shorthand. But it pleased me, somehow, that she did. While I waited for the drink I glanced around the garden, taking in a world most people in Manchester didn't know existed. The air here sparkled. I'd never seen such lush green grass. Everywhere I looked, I saw touches of understated elegance and class. It wasn't just the crystal, the china, the expensive booze, or the care with which the garden had been manicured. It was the ease with which the people here wore their lives. The people at that garden party were all the product of generations of success and power. The men were third-generation Ivy League. Their wives were Smith or Vassar. Whatever achievements they had or hadn't accomplished on their own, whatever joys or disappointments they'd faced in their private lives, they moved with a sense of confidence and purpose that I soon came to realize was based on a sense that their lives were built on a deep and solid foundation of family history. Every fine thing I saw at Max Smith's house was a celebration of the power of identity.

In the late 1960s, it was not considered cool for a brother from the ghetto to be taken with the fortunate genealogy of the steeplechase set over in Ligonier, but I had to admit, something about the power of all that personal history moved me. I wondered what it would feel like to stand on such an established past—I imagined it felt like bedrock beneath your feet.

The history of the folks in Manchester was a history of severed roots, broken families, and lost origins leading back to slave ships, not the *Mayflower,* and it would have been easy to see these Ligonier folks as my natural antagonists. But I liked what I saw here, and I saw no contradiction in that feeling. Why shouldn't we want some class, some tone, some fineness in our lives? Why should I have to apologize for thinking it was possible? Mr. Ross had allowed me to dream, but dreams are just fantasies unless they are rooted in a solid understanding of who you are. Ligonier gave me a new picture of how life could look and feel. I was already dreaming of how I could get myself some of that feeling back home in Manchester. Unlike my new Ligonier friends, I had no deep, distinguished history to shape me, but I knew that if I wanted a little of what they had, I'd need a firm foundation for my dreams, a clear sense of purpose and identity. If life hadn't given me those things, I'd have to find a way to create them on my own.

We ate steaks at a long table in the garden. After dessert, it was time for me to make my pitch. I told them how Frank Ross's art class had changed my life, and explained that the center I wanted to build would pass on the lessons he'd taught me. It would do more than teach kids to make pots, I said; it would be a place where kids could feel the power of positive experiences that would open the door to self-discovery, give them a sense of their own potential and a base from which they could dream. When I finished, the members of the vestry convened privately for a few moments, then Reverend Smith approached me and shook my hand.

"We like your ideas very much," he said. "This should help get you started."

And he handed me a check made out for ten thousand bucks.

WHEN BISHOP APPLEYARD heard that the meeting in Ligonier had been successful, he assigned his senior administrator, Father George Werner, to put me in touch with lawyers from Reed, Smith,

Shaw & McClay, the most prestigious law firm in the city, who walked me through the process of getting myself incorporated. Once that was accomplished, I was able to cash the check from St. Michael's. But the ten thousand dollars was just the beginning; since our meeting in Ligonier, St. Michael's vestry had decided to contribute tens of thousands of additional dollars. In the meanwhile, the bishop had been speaking with Father Jim Dix, the rector of Fox Chapel Episcopal Church in the affluent Pittsburgh suburb of Fox Chapel, whose congregation had agreed to match St. Michael's offer. Just like that, I found myself in charge of an annual operating budget of almost $25,000. Things were happening fast.

"You need a building," Tom told me. "The church owns a house you can use, but you better see it before you make a commitment." Tom and I drove to the house. It was on Buena Vista Street in Manchester, which, like most streets in the neighborhood, was lined with sullen brick row houses in various stages of disrepair. Tom stopped the car in front of one of the worst of them.

"That's it," he said.

The house Tom was pointing at was a disaster. Its brick walls were bulging. The small wooden porch seemed about to topple into the street. The windows were covered with plywood, and the battered front door hung cockeyed on its rusted hinges. Inside was even worse. The air reeked with foul dampness and rot. Plaster had fallen away from the filthy walls and ceilings in big ragged patches. Garbage was scattered everywhere, and the floors were lined with soiled mattresses used by the junkies who had claimed the place as a shooting gallery. With all the windows boarded up, the place was dark, even in broad daylight. There was no electricity, no heat, no running water.

"It's a total gut job," Tom said. "What do you think?"

I nodded. "We can make this work."

But I wasn't being overconfident. I already knew what to do with that place. It was a vision I'd had in my head for years and had made real, in a limited sense, in the basement of our house. While I was still in high school, I convinced my mother to let me transform our dingy basement into my own underground refuge. I wanted to capture in that space the healing, energizing atmosphere I'd found in Mr. Ross's classroom. In a matter of weeks, I gutted the walls to the studs, ran new wiring, hung fresh Sheetrock everywhere, and installed stylish track lights on the ceiling. Mr. Ross had made me a big fan of Frank Lloyd Wright's architecture, so I tried to use design principles and colors I saw in examples of his work to give my space an organic, architectural feel. When the construction was finished, I brought in a secondhand sofa and a thick shag rug, then set up a KLH stereo like the one in Mr. Ross's room and a coffeemaker just like his. My father bought me a 35-millimeter camera at a pawnshop, and I set up a small photo studio in the basement. With his help, I also built a makeshift potter's wheel out of parts we salvaged from the junkyard—some two-by-fours for the base, an old sewing machine motor, and, for the turntable, an abandoned manhole cover. It didn't look like much, but I made some nice pots on that ramshackle thing.

That basement retreat became my sanctuary. I spent hours down there, making pots, working with my photographs, reading the books on art and architecture I got from Mr. Ross, listening to the jazz albums he'd lend me, or just dreaming of all the places my life might lead. Having that space to escape to got me through some difficult times and gave me a sane, quiet place where I could explore the things that interested me, sort out what mattered most, and begin to imagine the kind of person I wanted to be. Along with Mr. Ross's classroom, that basement hideaway would make me a lifelong believer in the power of a positive environment. I knew that the environment I would create in the Buena Vista house would be an ambitious elaboration of that simple space, a place where kids could feel safe, feel important, and find some room to dream.

Construction began immediately. I enlisted my father as general contractor—he was out of work at the time—and except for the HVAC guys who put in the furnace, the two of us did all the work. We gutted the place from top to bottom, put in new plumbing, new bathroom fixtures, a new furnace, and new electrical service. We installed new doors and windows and hung fresh Sheetrock on all the walls. Frank Ross pitched in by helping me organize and track down all the equipment and supplies I'd need to run an art school. He also helped design an efficient layout for the studio, and when all the other work was done, he worked with my father and me to build a kiln in the basement. Before long, the bulk of the work was finished—the walls were painted, the wheels and worktables were set in place, tools were at hand, and a supply of clay was laid up in the storeroom. Next, I brought in my coffeemaker and set up the KLH. In the days before we opened, I spent some time alone in the renovated space, listening to jazz. I was happy with the changes we had made. The rot and filth had been stripped away. Everything was clean and sound, and sunlight streamed in through the windows. I christened the place the Manchester Craftsmen's Guild, because I was taken with the old European guild system in which masters passed on their skills and knowledge to young apprentices.

On the morning of our opening day, I made a pot of coffee, put some jazz on the KLH, unlocked the doors, and waited for my apprentices to arrive. I wish I could say they were lining up to get in, but in fact, most of Manchester hardly seemed to notice I was there. Some kids drifted in, played with the clay, drifted out again. It went on that way for days. I had to swallow my disappointment. Naively, I had expected kids to come in and fall in love with clay, the way I had, the first time they laid their hands on it. But it didn't happen that way.

So I started to work the streets to drum up some business. It was easy to get kids into the center for a lesson or two, but few of them showed up for classes on a regular basis. Even the most promising kids would lose interest and fail to show. But I never gave up on them. In those early days, I kept every kid who came into the place on my radar screen. I'd talk to them in the streets, coaxing them to come back. Sometimes, I'd track them down at their homes. Too often, I found them living in conditions of such disorder and neglect that it took my breath away.

"I've been hoping to see you at the Craftsmen's Guild," I'd tell them, wanting them to believe as truly as I did that the clay could turn their lives around. They'd make some excuse about being sick or being busy, but the truth of what they were thinking was in their eyes: *Look at my house. Look at my life. What is your school going to do for me?*

I was living in an apartment above the Craftsmen's Guild then, and sometimes, late at night when I couldn't sleep, I'd go into the studio, put on some jazz, and throw some pots. In those quiet hours, I realized I would have to amend my romantic view of my mission at the center. The young people of my neighborhood were being destroyed by rage, drugs, violence, apathy, fear, despair, and all the other devastating aspects of institutionalized poverty. I thought I could save them with the power of art. But that was *my* dream, not theirs. I couldn't expect them to buy into my vision just because I wanted them to. I wasn't going to save anyone who wasn't ready to be saved, and if I was expecting gratitude for what I was trying to do, I was on a fool's mission—the people I was trying to help hadn't asked me to help them, and they didn't owe me anything. All I could do was share what I had to share with whoever was willing to listen. When students showed up, I taught them how to make pots. When they didn't, I worked on pots of my own. And I spread the word about the Craftsmen's Guild every chance I got.

As months passed, I became a familiar and unlikely figure on the streets of Manchester, a six-foot-four-inch brother decked out in work boots and heavy twill workingman's slacks from the Army Navy Store, mingling with riot cops and Black Panthers, church folks and hoodlums, preaching a sermon about the power of art. In those troubled days, it was one of few messages in the neighborhood that had the power to unite. I remember one afternoon, for example, when the sun was shining and the studio was empty. On an impulse, I put my stereo speakers in the windows, put on some jazz, dragged a potter's wheel out onto the front porch of the Craftsmen's Guild, and started to work with clay. The kids were the first to notice me, and a bunch of them gathered around. Then a couple of neighborhood guys, hustlers, scam artists, stopped as they were passing by.

Next time I looked up, a couple of Black Panthers, decked out in berets, leather jackets, and shades, were watching from across the street. I asked one of the kids if he'd like to try his hand, and he nodded, so I loaded some fresh clay on the wheel and waved him up to the porch.

Just as he started to work, a police cruiser rolled by. Two cops were inside. The officer in the passenger seat had a shotgun resting between his knees.

"What's going on?" he asked.

"Making some pots, officer," I answered.

"That's Bill Strickland," said the policeman at the wheel. "The artist. He runs this place."

The cop with the shotgun nodded and looked me over. I felt the Panthers watching, too, and the street toughs, and I felt all the weight of all the tension that filled Manchester in those days pressing down hard on me. But then I looked down at the kid sitting at the potter's wheel. He was smiling, laughing, thinking about nothing but the clay. In that moment, none of the bad stuff could touch him; he was not afraid anymore, he wasn't angry or confused, he was just a kid being happy. The small crowd watched for a while as the boy on the porch tried to shape a spinning lump of clay. When it rose and slopped comically on its side, everybody laughed. When the squad car pulled away, the cop with the shotgun waved and nodded. He was still smiling.

There is power in this clay, I told myself as the squad car disappeared, and I hoped it was only a matter of time before other people believed that, too.

DURING THE MONTHS that I worked to get the Craftsmen's Guild off the ground, I was also struggling to keep my college career from veering off the tracks. My first semester ended in December, and the news wasn't good. I had managed only a C-minus average, which, by the terms of my probation, should have got me tossed out on my ear.

But after my impassioned pleas for mercy, the admissions people gave me one more semester to turn things around. I knew I had to find a way to get my bearings, and fast. So I made it my business to make friends with the smartest kids in my classes and find out what they knew that I didn't. I started by introducing myself to groups of students gathered in the dining hall or the student union. I drew them into conversations about classes and professors. I asked about their study habits and how they knew what to expect on tests. When I got to know them well enough, they let me study their notes from class. Sometimes we'd study together, and as I worked with them I realized what I'd been missing. From the moment I started at Pitt, I felt as if I'd been struggling to find my way through a blinding whirlwind. But my new friends were much more systematic in their approach. Where I saw chaos, they saw context and structure—one concept building upon another, one set of ideas laying the foundation for the next. I realized that college wasn't some monstrous guessing game, that there was a method to it all. Each class had an organizing context. The trick was to find that context, then use it as a framework to force order and meaning on the steady stream of themes and concepts. Once I saw that, everything changed. I listened to lectures with a more discriminating ear. My notes became more concise and effective. My questions grew more informed. I was finding my bearings, and as my confidence increased, I participated more eagerly in class discussions and felt more comfortable asking my professors for advice.

Still, I knew my fellow classmates had a huge head start on me, and the only way I could close that gap was to work harder than I'd ever worked before. I poured myself into my studies with an almost desperate sense of purpose, reading my textbooks two or three times and skimping on sleep to make sure I was ready for exams. It was a grueling experience, but my performance steadily improved, and when our grades came out at the end of the semester I was amazed to see I had worked my way onto the Dean's List. It was an exhilarating feeling. I had proven to myself I was up to the challenge of college. More important, I knew now that I could compete, at a high level, with the brightest kids around. I might have to work twice as hard, but I could do it. I could make it in the world outside of Manchester, and that meant I had a future. But my goal was not to find that future outside my neighborhood. My vision was to live a meaningful life right where I was, and for the time being, that meant making a success of the Craftsmen's Guild.

As the months passed and the weather grew colder, the racial tensions in Manchester eased a little and I took advantage of the calm to spread the news about the Craftsmen's Guild any way I could. I did pottery demonstrations at schools, neighborhood centers, and street festivals. I made presentations to churches and community groups. Whenever I could, I gave kids the chance to get their hands on some clay. Almost before I knew it, months turned into years, but gradually my promotional efforts paid off. More and more kids showed up for classes. More important, they stuck around long enough for the clay to make a difference, and at last, the magic I'd been waiting for started to happen. Kids stumbled on talents they never dreamed of. They surprised themselves with their ability to create. And they discovered the transforming power that comes when your work and skill and imagination result in the creation of a beautiful thing. I was giving them small tastes of success, as Frank Ross had given me. I was hoping that it would inspire them to seek out more of that good feeling in other areas of their lives. I wasn't disappointed. Soon, I began hearing from public school teachers that kids who came to the Crafts-men's Guild were showing a noticeable improvement at school: Their attendance was better, they seemed more focused and attentive, and they were getting better grades. Parents noticed the improvement too, and as word got around the neighborhood, more and more students showed up at my door. Soon, we were forced to add more wheels and more classes. Impressed with our progress, the Episcopal Church, along with other financial supporters we'd gathered along the way, had steadily increased our funding, until eventually I found myself with an operating budget of $75,000 a year.

A couple of years passed, and as the center continued to thrive, we decided to create a photography program, so I bought a vacant build-ing across the street—where the Black Panthers had had their head-quarters during the riots—and rehabbed it into a large photo studio. On the first day of classes, I handed all the kids a camera. I meant it as a show of trust, and most of the kids appreciated that. Unfortu-nately, my trust was not always warranted. More than once, a student would disappear for good, taking a camera with him. Once, I bumped into a photo student who hadn't been showing up for class. When he told me he wasn't coming back, I asked him what happened to his camera. He gave me a look of amused disbelief, shook his head, and walked away. I knew what he was thinking: *If you're fool enough to hand me a camera, that's your business, but your camera just bought me a bag of weed and a bottle of wine, man.* I ached for every kid I lost that way, but my experiences at the Craftsmen's Guild had long since taught me that I wasn't going to save every kid in Manchester. In fact, I now understood that saving other people wasn't my primary mission at all. I couldn't save anyone, in fact, until I saved myself, until I *knew* myself and knew what I wanted my life to be. I was only twenty-one years old. It wasn't that long ago that I'd been a troubled Manchester kid myself, defined and limited by low regard for my own potential and false assumptions about what the world had to offer a person like me. In those days, I would hear people speak about life as a journey, and meaning and fulfillment as if they were distant destinations. In Manchester, all the roads were dead ends or led to places I didn't want to go. If the kind of life I longed for lay off somewhere in the distance, it was hidden in some place I couldn't get to, on paths I couldn't find. I had felt defeated before my life had even begun.

But Frank Ross had shown me a better metaphor for life in a shapeless lump of clay. He taught me I could dream my future the same way I shaped a pot or vase, with vision, skill, and care. Watching the Manchester Craftsmen's Guild grow from a mere dream, *my* dream, into solid reality was proof that Mr. Ross was right. In just a few years, the Guild had become one of the brightest points of light in the neighborhood, a source of hope and direction for hundreds of disadvantaged kids, in its modest way helping to transform the world. But for all the good that came out of the place and all the lives that were touched, the person it helped the most was me. It gave me the space I needed to find out who I really am. Years before, I had envied those white folks in Ligonier for the deep roots that gave them such a solid foundation for their lives. But now I knew that identity isn't something you inherit, it's something you must discover. The Craftsmen's Guild was helping me discover mine. Who was I? I was the guy who believed that art and creative experience are stronger than fear and ignorance. I was the guy who created this place out of passion and vision and sweat. I built the Guild out of ideas and things I treasured, or needed, or believed in, and in doing so, I created the kind of personal foundation Frank Ross had talked about—a foundation crafted from genuine values and passions that would serve as a base for a rich and meaningful life.

The Craftsmen's Guild was, for me, proof of the power of a dream. But even as the Guild prospered, other dreams were coming true, as well. In 1972, I graduated, cum laude, from the University of Pittsburgh with a bachelor's degree in history. I was making great strides as a Pittsburgh ceramics artist, doing more shows at bigger venues and raising my profile in the local arts establishment. Through my work at the Craftsmen's Guild I had developed a network of influential friends and allies, and I had learned to move with confidence and effectiveness in the loftiest circles of Pittsburgh's power elite. I was no longer just some guy on the street. I was someone who mattered, someone who had built something of substance, meaning, and purpose, and I hadn't had to leave Manchester to do it. As a kid, I had seen the world as an obstacle course, full of danger, impassable barriers, and paths that only led back to where you started. Now I saw opportunities everywhere. I was beginning to realize that nothing is impossible if you have the vision, the courage, and the sheer stubbornness to open the doors to a dream.

One year after we opened the Craftsmen's Guild, I took a group of students to Ligonier, where they showed their ceramic art at the summer arts fair at St. Michael's Church. My kids were the hit of the show. They watched as important-looking white folks crowded around our display to express their admiration for the work my kids had done. I knew what it felt like to them to be taken seriously in a place like Ligonier, to be seen as someone who came there not as a victim, not as someone in need or asking for a favor, but someone with something beautiful to show, something valuable to share, some powerful story to tell. It was a perfect summer day, and horses were out in the pastures as we drove home.

"Keep these pictures in your head," I told the kids. "Keep this feeling with you."

CHAPTER FOUR

Expanding Our Mission

J ust after graduating from the University of Pittsburgh, I caught wind of a job opening at the Bidwell Training Center, a job-training program in Manchester that opened its doors in 1968, at about the same time I founded the Craftsmen's Guild. Bidwell's mission was to school poor folks in the building trades—carpentry, masonry, electricity, and plumbing—but like many inner-city jobs programs at the time, it had never lived up to expectations. According to rumors in the neighborhood, managers at Bidwell, who favored designer suits and flashy jewelry, and who cruised the streets in late-model luxury cars, were lining their pockets with the state and federal grant money intended to support the school, while the quality of instruction floundered. I didn't know much about Bidwell—or the building trades, for that matter—but I did notice that a lot of Bidwell graduates were turning up behind the counter at McDonald's and Burger King. So, when the crew who ran the place was finally let go, I drew up a proposal for turning Bidwell around and threw my hat in the ring.

The training center was founded by the Bidwell Presbyterian Church, and I was interviewed for the job at the home of the church's minister, Reverend James Robinson, by the reverend himself and an associate.

"Do you have a college degree?" the minister asked.

I handed them a copy of my résumé. "I just graduated from Pitt with a B.A. in history," I said.

He glanced at the résumé and nodded.

"Have you paid your income taxes?" he asked.

The question caught me by surprise. I didn't know it at the time, but Bidwell's previous managers had allowed the school's taxes to fall into arrears to the tune of $300,000. The minister smiled when I assured him I always paid my taxes on time.

"We know about your work at the Craftsmen's Guild," the minister said, "and we're delighted that you're interested in our position. When can you start?"

I glanced involuntarily at my briefcase, which contained the proposal I never got to present. "I got the job?" I asked.

"It's yours if you want it."

I told them that I did want the job, but only on condition that I could continue running the Craftsmen's Guild as well. They didn't bat an eye. Then we worked out the details of salary and benefits without a hitch. In what seemed like the wink of an eye, I walked out of their office with a new title, a new salary, a new future, and a sense that it had all come way too easily. A few days later, when I stood in Bidwell's parking lot and took my first look at the place, I began to wonder what I'd taken on. Bidwell's home was a sagging brick warehouse set in a seedy North Side parking lot. Half the windows were broken. Weeds were growing up through cracks in the pavement and shrubs were growing wild. On one side of the building I saw a young man crouching in the weeds—one of my students, I presumed—sticking a needle into his arm. More young men were gathered at the building's entrance, smoking dope and shooting dice on the sidewalk. They barely acknowledged my presence as I made my way past them and walked through the front door. I stepped into a small reception area. The space was as cramped and oppressive as a cave. Old linoleum tile, scarred and peeling, covered the floor. The walls were clad with fake wood paneling so thin and cheap it bowed out from the studs. The only light came from dim fluorescent fixtures set into the dropped acoustical ceiling. Some of the ceiling tiles showed old brown water stains. Others were missing, and I could see the peeling paint and crumbling plaster of the original ceiling above. I nodded to a woman sitting at a metal desk in a makeshift reception area. She was wearing sweat clothes, had bedroom slippers on her feet, and was eating what looked to be a bowl of collard greens. She nodded back but kept on eating, so I showed myself around.

All the rooms and hallways were just as bleak and dingy as the small lobby. I wandered in and out of windowless classrooms and dreary offices. In the bathrooms I found leaking pipes and backed-up toilets. The bare wooden stairway that led to the second-floor hallway creaked and shifted as I climbed it, and when I walked down the hallway the floor sloped so dramatically beneath the cheap carpet that I almost walked into a wall. Everywhere I looked I saw signs of neglect and incompetence: water damage from the leaking roof, doors so out of square they couldn't be closed, ugly rough patches on walls where crumbling plaster had been amateurishly repaired, torn carpeting, exposed wiring, cracked tiles, peeling paint. This was a place that claimed to be preparing students for jobs in the building trades? It was clear to me at that point that the rumors had been true—the previous managers had plundered Bidwell's budget, fattening their own wallets and letting the school become a hovel. But after only a few weeks at Bidwell's helm, I realized that the deplorable physical condition of the place was only part of the problem. The shameless negligence and abuses that marked the previous administration's management had fostered a culture of cynicism, mistrust, and disrespect that was so deeply rooted in Bidwell's DNA it was almost pathological. The place was lawless. Drug deals went down in the hallways. Junkies would overdose in the johns. Vandalism and theft were rampant and often stunningly bold. One night, just a few weeks after I took the job, some crook—who turned out to be one of our students—sledgehammered his way through a cinder-block exterior wall and almost made off with all our electronic typewriters; we found them lined up in the hallway and could only assume he was interrupted before he could haul them away. A short time later, another burglar broke in and ripped the copper plumbing out of the walls. Our students showed up for classes armed with every kind of concealed weapon, and violent confrontations were common. But it wasn't just the students who were the problem. The madness of Bidwell infected faculty members, too, as I learned one morning when I pulled into the parking lot and saw one of our counselors sighting down the barrel of a hunting rifle at a Bidwell student who was racing toward me for cover. I jumped out of the car and waved my arms. When the counselor saw me, he lowered the weapon.

"What's going on?" I called out.

"Kid pissed me off!" the counselor shouted.

For a moment, the surreal nature of the situation struck me dumb. Then I heard myself crying out, "You can't shoot the students, man!"

I realized, with a painful clarity, just what I was up against. My experience at the Craftsmen's Guild had convinced me that respect breeds respect, that high expectations lead to higher achievement. Now I found myself running a school where the roof leaked, the walls leaned, the toilets didn't work, and the floor wasn't even level. What greater disrespect could we show them? Everything about Bidwell screamed with contempt for the very students it was founded to assist. Why should they trust us? The school was sending them the same old dehumanizing message they'd been hearing all their lives: *You have no future. Your life doesn't matter. What you see around you is all you deserve.* At the Craftsmen's Guild, I'd found what I thought was a powerful answer to that lie, to the lie that can undercut every one of our lives. If others don't value us, or see our potential and encourage it, how can we value and make the most of ourselves? Doesn't matter where we live or how we are raised. Here our disregard was hanging over the kids like a toxic cloud. I knew I wouldn't last long in that environment. So, on a Friday afternoon just before closing, I called the staff together and told them their lives were about to change.

"We need to clean this place up," I said, "so you're all invited to a painting party this weekend. I'll buy the paint and the beer. You're all expected; anyone who doesn't show up is fired." They thought I was kidding until the next afternoon when I counted heads and discovered one staff member missing. I publicly fired him in absentia (I fired him for real the following Monday), and that got their attention. The paint didn't make much of an improvement, but I had made my presence known. I had also made a statement: *We aren't going to live like this or treat our kids this way anymore.*

I meant every word of it, but I knew I couldn't make that happen on my own. What I needed was a strong partner to help me refine and implement my vision, and fight all the battles that lay ahead. The guy I wanted was Jesse Fife, a friend I'd made in college. Jesse was one year behind me at Pitt and the only other African-American student in the History Department. Like me, he had been raised on Pittsburgh's North Side, and like me, he had struggled to steer his life in a positive direction. From the start, Jesse struck me as a stable, responsible, highly intelligent young man with deep reserves of integrity and quiet strength. He also had a strong sense of responsibility to the community, and a conviction that his own success should do some good for the people around him. I liked him and respected him immediately, and we soon formed a friendship that is still going strong today. Hiring Jesse was the best move I could have made. His talents and temperament perfectly complemented mine. He had a lucid, pragmatic way of thinking that slowed down my characteristically urgent intensity and gave balance and direction to my impulses. He also had a brilliant knack for taking on my dreams as his own, then dealing with the practical, logistical hurdles that had to be overcome to make those dreams come true. Like me, Jesse was short on business credentials and teaching experience, and we both worked by the seat of our pants for a while, learning the ropes as we groped our way forward, but from the moment he teamed up with me, Jesse was an essential component of all the success we've enjoyed.

It took some convincing to get Jesse on board—the first time I showed him the Bidwell Center from the parking lot he laughed, cried out, "No way, Bill!" and headed back for the car. But I told him I was determined to turn Bidwell into a source of hope for the same poor people we'd both grown up with, a place that could change people's lives, and that I needed his help to be successful. I understood that he had other options at the time that most likely would have led him to an easier, more lucrative career, but I truly believed that Bidwell, for all its flaws and the challenges it presented, was a place where Jesse belonged. Eventually, he saw it that way too, and accepted my offer. In appreciation, I bought him a Brooks Brothers suit, then set him up in an office near mine, and in the following months and years, Jesse and I did our best to change the culture at Bidwell. I hired better teachers, upgraded the quality of instruction, and raised the standards for student performance. But as long as we were housed where we were, I could never accomplish what really needed to be done—kill what Bidwell had always been and reinvent the place as a center of hope and pride. To do that, I needed to create an environment at Bidwell that offered our students a compelling alternative to the self-destructive logic of the streets. That would take a carefully plotted strategy implemented over a period of years. I knew from the get-go I didn't have the time or the money to pull that off. The bulk of Bidwell's budget came from state and federal grants, supplemented by money from local foundations and corporate givers. All of that funding was maddeningly erratic. It could disappear in the wink of an eye, depending on a shift in the political winds, or in the personal preference of whatever corporate officer was writing us checks. A huge portion of my energy was spent in the constant pursuit of funding. But despite my efforts, we survived hand-to-mouth, scrambling every day just to keep the doors open. The pressures of simple survival forced me to keep my sights focused on whatever immediate financial crisis was at hand. I never had the luxury of looking far enough ahead to develop a vision for the future. Working that way left me in a state of almost constant frustration, and as time passed, it became very clear to me that unless I built a better funding base for Bidwell I'd spend the rest of my time there just trying to keep my head above water. I never stopped trying to establish such a base, but more often than not my efforts led to demoralizing failures.

In 1976, for example, I began a series of talks with the city of Pittsburgh to win Bidwell the financial support of city hall. As part of those talks, the mayor sent a team of representatives to meet with me at Bidwell. We were gathered in my office, a windowless room in the back of the building at the end of a long, gloomy hallway. We had just convened the meeting when the lights went out. A moment later, someone in the hallway yelled, *"Fire!"* The emergency lighting didn't come on, and with no natural light in my office, we were plunged into absolute darkness. I told everyone to sit tight, then I groped my way around the desk, found the mayor's people, and led them out of the office and down the dark hallway to the stairwell that led to safety. Firefighters responded quickly and the fire was contained before the place burned down.

The fire marshal who investigated the blaze was a North Side guy who knew my family from the neighborhood.

"Did you find the cause?" I asked when he'd finished the investigation.

He nodded. "The service panel was wired improperly," he said. "Looks like some amateur did it." He didn't have to point out the obvious irony, that the administrators of a building trades school—a school that purports to train professional electricians—couldn't even have their own walls wired safely. The message was clear to the mayor's people, too, and the deal with the city soon fell apart. But there was worse news than that. The fire marshal's investigation had turned up a raft of serious safety violations.

"You don't have fire escapes," he told me. "You have offices and classrooms with no windows and no means of escape. Your fire extinguishers don't work. And then there's this."

He handed me a slender chrome cylinder, which I recognized as one of the ceiling nozzles of the building's sprinkler system. "I reached up to inspect it," he said, "and it came loose in my hand. It was stuck to the acoustical tile with glue. None of these nozzles are connected to the plumbing."

Another flimflam of the previous owners—they had probably pocketed the money for the sprinkler system, leaving everyone in the school at risk. I explained to the fire marshal that I knew nothing about and had nothing to do with that scam, but he wasn't moved.

"This place is a firetrap," he barked. "If you weren't Evelyn Strickland's son, I'd throw your ass in jail." Instead, he wrote me up for operating a dangerous facility and sent us to court. Fortunately, the judge who heard the case was someone who knew me and respected what I had done at the Craftsmen's Guild. He didn't shut us down, but he did order us to move to a safer facility and gave us forty-five days to do so. Soon after the verdict, I got a call from the federal official who oversaw the funding granted to us by the U.S. Labor Department. He wasn't in the mood to show us any mercy.

"I heard about the judge's decision," he said. "I have no choice but to dock your funding for every day you're closed." We couldn't afford that financial hit, so I called the staff together and began to organize a move. In just a few weeks, we found another warehouse nearby that was marginally less derelict than the one we were leaving behind. But it did meet all the required safety standards, and it fit our meager budget. We couldn't afford professional movers—the lowest bid I got was $30,000 and that was way beyond our means—so I rented a couple of trucks, and with the help of our staff and some willing students, we emptied the contents of the 40,000-square-foot warehouse ourselves—all the furniture and equipment in our offices and classrooms, all the tools and gear in our workshops and storage areas, all our materials and supplies—and, in the space of one furious weekend, moved it all to the new building on our own. We started when the school closed on a Friday afternoon. By Monday morning, we were in the new facility and open for business. Then I called the Labor Department to tell my liaison there that I had saved him the trouble and paperwork of cutting off my money.

We settled into our new space quickly and soon realized that the problems that had hounded us at our previous address had followed us into our new home. I spent my time writing grant proposals and chasing after funding. At the same time, the slumping economy raised unemployment everywhere, making jobs in the building trades harder and harder to come by. Was I going through all of this for nothing, training students for jobs that didn't exist? It was painfully obvious that Bidwell needed a dramatically new vision if it was going to become a place that could truly transform lives. I didn't know what Bidwell needed to be, but I had a sense that the answer was somewhere in the wind, so as I labored day to day to win the short-term funding that would keep Bidwell operating at status quo, I kept a desperate eye peeled for signs that might lead to our future. It was a long time coming, and more than once I almost lost heart, but finally a sign appeared in the shape of a new electric typewriter from IBM.

We needed new typewriters at the school, so I met with an IBM sales rep who made an impressive case for a new line of electronic typewriters called Selectrics. These new machines were so superior to anything else on the market, he said, that they would soon be standard equipment in offices across the country. "I'll take the typewriters," I said, "but there's a condition. I want to meet the guy who runs IBM operations in this region." I had no clear reason for making that condition except a vague intuition that a contact at a company like IBM couldn't help but improve Bidwell's fortunes. A few weeks later, I was giving IBM executive Ed Conrad a tour of our operation. He and I hit it off. He was able to see beyond what Bidwell was and understand what I wanted it to be.

When he had seen enough of me and Bidwell, I asked him to join my board of directors, and he accepted. I was elated. I knew that an official association with IBM would give Bidwell's credibility a badly needed boost. I had also become convinced that Ed was a link to a new world of possibilities, and that he could make me a part of a conversation about emerging technologies and the job markets of the future that might show me a way to reinvent Bidwell. Ed soon became an important part of the Bidwell scene, and it wasn't long before our association began to pay off. Ever since I'd talked to the IBM sales rep, I'd been thinking about the Selectrics. If they sold as well as he expected them to, businesses would need expert typists trained to get the most out of these sophisticated machines. So I suggested that Bidwell and IBM collaborate to develop a training program that would turn out typists specifically prepared to master the Selectrics. IBM

liked the idea, and soon the program was up and running. By the time
the first students graduated from our new typing program, the IBM
sales rep's prediction had come true—Selectrics had become the typewriter of choice in offices across the country, and we were able to
place our students in jobs everywhere.

The success of our typing program was a badly needed victory, but
we had no time to pat ourselves on our backs. Our conversations with
IBM had tipped us off to yet another emerging opportunity. In the
late 1970s and early '80s, computers were becoming an important
part of the American business scene. Data had to be entered into these
computers by qualified employees. We decided that with IBM's help,
we would design a keypunch program that would train students to
take advantage of this burgeoning field. The program was another wild
success: Businesses lined up to hire our graduates, and we couldn't
train them fast enough.

We scored another hit a few years later when Jesse walked into my
office one morning with a newspaper in his hand and a hunch about
another technological trend that would provide us with another key
opportunity, the arrival of cable television.

"Did you see the paper?" Jesse said to me. "This cable thing is going
to be big."

Warner Cable had just won the contract to supply the entire city
of Pittsburgh with cable TV services. As part of the deal, Warner had
agreed to cut the black community in by donating shares of their
stock to selected neighborhood groups and social service agencies,
including the Bidwell Training Center.

"You should talk to these people," Jesse said. "This could mean a
lot of jobs."

A few days later, I called an executive at Warner Cable and introduced myself. "Thanks for the stocks," I told him. "Stocks are cool, but I want to know who's going to build your cable system."

"We haven't figured that out yet," he answered. "We'll need to train a lot of people."

"What if we train them for you?" I said. He was open to the idea, so Jesse set to work on a proposal, working out all the logistical details concerning faculty, curriculum, supplies, equipment, and so on. When the Warner execs saw the program Jesse had put together, they decided that we were, indeed, the people to train their new workforce. Before long, trainees were practicing their climbing skills on the forest of telephone poles Jesse had planted in the asphalt of our parking lot, and learning to string and splice cable in our classrooms. With the help of one of Warner's senior technicians—who became a full-time faculty member at Bidwell—Jesse was able to set up the program that trained the small army of technicians who built the first citywide cable TV system in Pittsburgh, providing our students with skills that remained marketable long after the initial infrastructure was in place.

Our successes with IBM and Warner convinced me that we had, at last, found the blueprint for Bidwell's future. The problem with most job-training programs, and the reason the vast majority of them failed, was that they were equipping people with skills that were behind the curve, preparing them for jobs in stale or overcrowded fields where stiff competition—not to mention the realities of racial prejudice—put them at a disadvantage. By spotting emerging opportunities, like the ones at IBM and Warner, we could design new programs, preferably in partnership with companies that would hire the people those programs would produce. It would give our students something they had never had—a flat-out, head-to-head advantage in the job market. We were going to put poor people at the cutting edge. That was the vision I had been searching for. That was how Bidwell would become a place that could truly transform lives. But I was about to learn an essential lesson about the relationship between vision and success: I saw that while vision is a crucial aspect of achievement, it gets you nowhere unless you have the dogged tenacity to make your vision real. This was represented to me in extraordinary fashion by George Fechter who chaired our board during those difficult days. His refusal to accept failure was an inspiring example to me, and it helped to prepare me for the long struggle that lay ahead. And there was no shortage of struggles back then. My dream was clear.

Unfortunately, because of the realities of Bidwell's financial needs, it was a dream that rested almost entirely in the hands of the cautious politicians and bureaucrats whose decisions shaped our future. It was a frustrating period of my life. I knew what I had to do, but I needed money to do it right, and in the early 1980s money for inner-city causes was harder than ever to find. When Ronald Reagan took office in 1981, funding for social programs was slashed across the board, and Bidwell did not escape the ax. State money dried up, too, and we soon found ourselves in desperate financial straits. I turned to the Pittsburgh corporate community for help, but too many corporations had been burned in the sixties and seventies by social programs that failed disastrously because of incompetent leadership or because they were outright scams. No one was willing to take a chance on us, despite our recent successes.

I felt my spirit shrinking as my dreams seemed to turn to lead, and I began to feel once again, as I had as a boy, before I met Frank Ross, that everything fine and meaningful in life just wasn't meant for me. I tried to conjure up the sense of life and joy I felt when I walked into Frank's classroom. But I couldn't find it. My mood turned dark. I was difficult to be around. I had to force myself to show up at the office. The only place I felt like myself was in the dim light of the Shamrock Inn, a neighborhood bar. Drinking at the Shamrock took the edge off my disappointment and temporarily eased the pain. And there were people like me there who knew what life could do to you. They always listened to my story, they never judged me, and I sought out the comfort of their company more and more often, at any time of day. Walking into the Shamrock started to feel like coming home. There was jazz on the jukebox, a friendly face most times, and a chance for some laid-back conversation. It gave me a place to hide and heal as I drifted down, waiting to touch bottom.

Bidwell's financial problems grew progressively worse, and at the beginning of December 1982, Jesse sat down with me and spelled out what we both already knew: Barring some miracle, we wouldn't make that month's payroll. For the next few weeks, we worked furiously to find some stopgap funding. But it became clear that we weren't going to make it, so we did the painful math and saw no other option but to let one-third of our workforce go. One morning, about a week before Christmas, I called the staff together and announced the layoffs. Then I headed to the Shamrock and drank four martinis for lunch. When I returned to the school, I closed my office door and sat alone, staring at the wall. I'd been spiraling down toward this moment for months. Now that it was here, I was overwhelmed with a sense of loss and self-recrimination.

How did you let this happen? I asked myself. *You've been treading water for fifteen years. You let yourself become a miserable grant writer, going door to door with your hat in your hand. You let the powers that be define you, man, you let them decide what is and isn't possible. You need to stand for something. You need to make a difference in people's lives.*

I glanced out my window at a barren plot of land about the size of a football field. Streets and houses once had occupied that land, but the houses were torched during the riots of 1968, leaving behind an abandoned patch of weeds and mud that was being used as a makeshift parking lot for a small fleet of tractor-trailers. It was a view that had always depressed me, and it reminded me, in some way, of the ultimate futility of my mission at Bidwell. But now, as I gazed down on that sorry mess, I was startled by a vision. I saw a sleek, hip, low-slung building, earth-toned, honeycombed with windows and skylights, and bathed in a golden light. I had seen that light before. When I was a high school senior, Frank Ross took some of us to visit Fallingwater, Frank Lloyd Wright's residential masterpiece in the heavily wooded mountains southeast of Pittsburgh. We parked in a gravel lot and walked along a path to the house. I was stunned when the house came into view. The structure straddles a waterfall, and despite the cantilevered levels that float like a stack of concrete trays over the streambed below, it sits in an almost magical harmony with the woodlands that surround it. It was that harmony that struck me, and the pale, pristine light that gathered around the house like an aura. To my young mind, that light represented everything that was missing from my life in Manchester at the time. It meant hope and possibility. I remember thinking, *If I could find that light in Manchester, everything would be all right.* That was nearly forty years ago. Now, in my moment of despair, I was seeing the light again, or feeling it in my heart. And I knew what I needed to do. I would build a new center bathed in that light. I'd create a space where I could gather together everything whole and healing I had ever known in my life, where I could make myself whole and, out of that wholeness, maybe do some *real* good for the people who were counting on my help.

If I'd let myself, I could easily have dismissed that vision as a mere mirage. For starters, where would I find the money for such an elaborate structure? I could barely raise enough cash to keep a sorry place like Bidwell limping along. Even if funding was available, how could powerful people be convinced to build such a beautiful place in the ghetto? And if, by some extraordinary chain of events, someone decided that the building I'd imagined deserved to be built, what had I accomplished that would lead them to believe I was the one to build it? If any of those thoughts occurred to me, they occurred as whispers on the fringes of my consciousness. I ignored them. I couldn't afford to be discouraged. My vision was too vivid to be dismissed. There had to be a way to make it happen. I knew it would be extraordinarily difficult and that I'd meet resistance at every turn, but I had no choice. If I was to have any chance of being the kind of person I wanted to be, of living the life I knew was possible, then I had to make that building real. The first step, I decided, was to find someone to give substance to my dream.

SEVERAL WEEKS LATER, I was sitting in the office of Tasso Katselas, one of Pittsburgh's leading architects. I'd first heard of him in high school, while doing an architectural critique for Mr. Ross on the monastery Katselas had built at St. Vincent's College in nearby Latrobe. I told Mr. Katselas about the critique and that I was impressed with his design. It expressed in what I thought was a fresh and effective way the philosophy of Frank Lloyd Wright.

"You're a Frank Lloyd Wright fan?" he asked.

"He's a hero to me," I said.

Katselas said, "Let me show you something." He lifted a framed photograph off a shelf behind his desk and handed it to me. I recognized Katselas as a younger man standing next to a distinguished older gentleman with wavy white hair.

"That's you, with Frank Lloyd Wright."

"I studied with him at Taliesin," Katselas said.

I stared at the photo for a long time. Then I started talking.

"Tasso," I said, "I don't have a dime, man, but I need you to design a building for me. I need a model, something I can show people. And I need it *now.*"

I knew in my heart that if the architect could capture in his model what I'd seen in my vision, somehow the vision would become real. So I described the place I had envisioned.

"I can do it," he said. "But it will cost ten thousand dollars."

"Do it," I said. "Send me a bill."

TASSO HAD THE MODEL for me a few weeks later. When I saw it, it took my breath away. Tasso had turned my vision into a tangible reality. I took it straight to Bidwell and set it on Jesse's desk.

"What's this?" he asked. I hadn't told Jesse of my vision, of my plan, for fear it would evaporate into thin air before I was able to make it concrete.

"Our new home," I said. "And we're going to build it right over there," I added, pointing out Jesse's window at the barren plot that had inspired my vision. Jesse had the same ugly view I did.

"What are you talking about?"

"I'm talking about a new center. We're going to move out of this hellhole and put Bidwell and the Craftsmen's Guild under one roof. Look at it. It's going to be the hippest damn inner-city training center in the world."

Jesse gave his head a worried shake. "Are you kidding me, man?" he said. "We can't even make payroll. How are you going to build this?"

"We have to build this."

Jesse studied the model. "How much did this thing cost?" he asked.

"Ten thousand bucks," I said.

"We don't *have* ten thousand bucks," Jesse protested, his voice thin and high, almost a falsetto.

"We'll find it. But we're going to need a lot more than that. The architect says it's going to cost five million dollars to build this."

Jesse fell back in his chair and laughed. "Where are we going to get that kind of money?"

I had no answer to that question, but I knew I had to find the funding. My survival depended on it. If I was going to live a life that made any kind of sense to me, I had no choice but to make that building happen.

It took about two weeks of preaching to win Jesse over, but once he embraced the idea he became just as determined as me to make it happen. And with his backing, I hit the streets with fire in my eyes. I lugged my model to the boardrooms of major corporations and foundations across the city. Everywhere I went, I met with the same dubious stares.

"You want to build this in Manchester?" someone would say.

"I'm *going* to build this in Manchester," I'd quietly answer.

There would be a delicate pause.

"Isn't this a little elaborate for a poverty center?" someone would ask.

"It's not a poverty center," I'd answer. "It's a center for success."

"How much will it cost to build it?" someone would ask.

"Five million," I'd say.

"Come on, Bill," the person would chuckle, "Manchester doesn't need a Taj Mahal."

"But Manchester needs this," I'd say, and I let everyone see I was serious. These guys all thought they knew me. I was the do-gooder from over on the North Side. As long as I was doing my thing at Bidwell and the Craftsmen's Guild in ways that suited their understanding of what was sensible and appropriate, they were happy to support me. Now it must have seemed to them that I was stepping out of my league, and I could see in their faces that it worried them a little. Still, I had enough of a track record by then, and had earned the respect of a sufficient number of important people, that they didn't want to turn me down flat. So, one by one, each corporation offered me a conditional pledge, which they would release to me only if I found matching money. The total of all those conditional pledges was three million dollars. It was pretty clear to me that few of the people in those boardrooms thought I had any chance of raising the matching funds. After all, where could I find that kind of money if I didn't get it from them?

Fortunately, my years at Bidwell and the Craftsmen's Guild had allowed me to build an extensive network of friends and supporters that included some powerful and influential people. One of them was Diana Jannetta, a socially prominent arts advocate who was at the time the chair of the Pennsylvania Arts Council. I was on the council, too, thanks to my work at the Craftsmen's Guild. Diana and I had become friends. Diana had always believed in my work, and she was one of the first to get behind my campaign to build a new center. I told her about the conditional grants I'd secured, but I confessed my doubts that I'd be able to raise the three million I needed to match the offers.

"Let's see if the governor can help," Diana said. It turned out that Diana was a friend of Dick Thornburgh, who was then the governor of Pennsylvania. A single call to the governor's mansion did the trick. A few weeks later, I found myself sitting in an opulent waiting room outside the governor's office with my cardboard model on my lap. Diana had made the trip with me, and was now meeting privately with the governor to talk me up and help make my case. When the door opened and they waved me in, I laid the model on the governor's desk and let him look it over. He smiled approvingly and asked a few questions, but I sensed he had already made up his mind.

"You think you can make this place work?" he asked.

"Yes, Governor," I said, "I do."

"Then stick out your hand," he said. "You're going to get your center."

A few weeks later, Jesse walked into my sorry little office at Bidwell and laid a check on my desk. It was made out in the amount of one and a half million dollars, with the balance due later.

"Look at those zeros!" Jesse cried.

"Hand me the phone," I said. "I have to call our corporate friends and tell them we'll be able to make use of their generosity after all."

Of course, that money wasn't the Governor's to give; the state legislature had to approve the funding before that money was released, and we were assisted in that regard by a man named K. Leroy Irvis, a powerful Pennsylvania politician, and a man I consider to be my spiritual godfather. Mr. Irvis, a state representative from Pittsburgh, would eventually become Speaker of the House, making him the first black speaker of any state legislature in the country. When we were trying to build the new center, he was house majority leader, and he used that clout to make sure state lawmakers followed through on the governor's commitment. But that wasn't the first time Mr. Irvis had come to our aid. He had been like a father to Jesse and me since those difficult early days at the Bidwell Training Center, and more than once his powerful intercession kept the doors open there when financial pressures threatened to pull us under. In December 1982, when we couldn't make the payroll at Bidwell and I had to lay off a third of the staff, Mr. Irvis drove to the center in a howling snowstorm to work out an arrangement that allowed me to keep the place afloat. He saved us again in 1995, long after the new center had been built, when our operations outgrew our state and federal funding, and I saw the very real possibility that I'd have to shut the place down.

We were fortunate at the time to have on our board a man named Bill Lieberman, a leading figure in Pittsburgh's corporate community whose business activities had earned him a string of political connections across the state. Bill, one of the most influential figures in Manchester Bidwell's history, was instrumental in helping me see that effective programs and good intentions weren't enough to ensure our survival. Too many worthy social programs had failed, he said, because their leaders depended upon the support of a political base that was too narrow. If we wanted to sustain and expand our vision for Manchester Bidwell over the long haul, he insisted, it was our responsibility to reach out to political figures and circles of power that might not seem to be natural supporters of programs like ours. In other words, if we wanted to win the kind of political support that could secure our future, we needed to convince powerful state legislators that our organization merited their support no matter what their political persuasion. It took some effort for Bill to convince us that such bilateral support was even possible, but once I saw the wisdom of it, Bill's insight became a huge influence on the way I thought about our future, and, in retrospect, I see it was a key element in all our subsequent growth and success.

Bill's way of thinking dovetailed perfectly with Mr. Irvis's approach, and with Bill's assistance, Mr. Irvis soon won the support of two important state representatives—John Purcell and Dwight Evans, who both served on the state house appropriations committee. John Purcell was a white Republican, Dwight Evans a black Democrat, and both men represented districts in the Philadelphia area, which lies about three hundred miles east of Pittsburgh. It was a testimony to Mr. Irvis's political sway, and to the personal respect he commanded, that he was able to pull them aboard the Manchester Bidwell bandwagon. At Mr. Irvis's recommendation, the two men sponsored legislation that increased the level of state funding for our organization, and made that funding a perennial item in the state's annual budget, giving us a new lease on life at a crucial point in our development and allowing us to grow into the enterprise we are today.

Mr. Irvis remained a staunch champion for Manchester Bidwell until his death in 2006 at the age of eighty-nine. Still, for all the political assistance he gave me, it's the personal relationship we shared that I treasure most. Despite the difference in our ages, we understood each other in an intuitive way that made me feel very close to him, and we shared interests and sensibilities that gave us a strong common bond. Mr. Irvis was a gifted wood sculptor. He wrote poetry, he built and flew model planes. He had devoted his entire political career to doing good for ordinary people, and was revered for it, but there was work he'd left undone. I think he saw in me an extension of himself, someone who could bring expression to the hopes and dreams he hadn't been able to make real. So he did everything he could to help me realize my dreams, and that made all the difference. Without Mr. Irvis's strong support and guidance, I wouldn't be who I am, and Manchester Bidwell as we now know it simply wouldn't exist.

WE BROKE GROUND for the new building in 1984, on that barren plot of land outside my office window. Construction was completed two years later, and Manchester Bidwell was born. Touring the finished building was a remarkable experience for me. My dream, which was based on nothing more substantial than a hunger for meaning and purpose and the most outrageous, impossible kind of hope, had been turned into literal reality. I was now walking around inside of it. Everything about the place—the sculptural dimensions of the exterior design; the interior rhythms of proportion and scale; the color and texture of the walls, floors, and fabrics; and that uplifting quality of light—was exactly what I had hoped it would be. I felt in my heart that we had done what we set out to do, to create an environment that had the power to transform lives. The mere idea of the place had power; we'd already seen proof of that power before construction had even begun.

When I was making the rounds of corporate offices with my cardboard model, trying to raise the money to build my dream, I met with a lot of skepticism and doubt, and even some condescension. But as word of what I was trying to do spread through the corporate community, there were those who saw potential in my vision.

One of them was Elsie Hillman, a prominent philanthropist in Pittsburgh, and a powerful political leader in the Republican Party at both the state and national levels. Elsie was one of our earliest and most influential supporters, and her endorsement of our efforts sent a clear signal to powerful people across Pittsburgh, throughout Pennsylvania, and even in the nation's capital that Manchester Bidwell was a place to be taken seriously. Having Elsie as an ally also broadened our base of support by helping me reach across the street to important Republican leaders who, according to conventional wisdom, may not have seemed to be the natural supporters of a place like Manchester Bidwell but who, over time, would prove to be a key reason for our success.

None of those leaders was more important than John Heinz, a U.S. senator who was at the time heir to the Heinz family assets, which included the Pittsburgh-based Heinz Company, makers of a very famous ketchup.

"I like what you're trying to do," Senator Heinz told me after summoning me to his office, "and we want to be part of it. As you know, we're trying to improve our minority hiring efforts at Heinz. You could help us a lot if you'd include a food-training program at your new facility."

I told the senator that I didn't think I could help him. "We've been teaching building trades, mostly," I said. "I'd be reluctant to take on a new field, especially one I know nothing about."

The senator nodded patiently. "What if we kicked in a million dollars and the full-time services of the head of our research department?" he asked.

I paused. "Well, Mr. Heinz," I replied slowly, "it looks like we're going into the food-service business!"

That conversation led directly to the birth of our culinary arts program. The money from the Heinz Company and the Heinz Foundation bought us state-of-the-art commercial facilities, and the expertise of Heinz chefs helped us shape a curriculum that virtually guaranteed our graduates good-paying jobs, not only as food technicians at Heinz but also as assistant chefs at restaurants throughout the city. We modeled our kitchens after the famed Culinary Institute of America in Hyde Park, New York, with invaluable advice from noted chef Paul Prudhomme. John Heinz became a personal friend, and he remained a strong supporter of Manchester Bidwell until his tragic death in an airplane crash in April 1991. (After John's death, his colleague Alfred W. "Burr" Wishart, then head of the Heinz Foundation, made sure the Foundation followed through on John's commitments, and soon became one of the most trusted and reliable members of the Manchester Bidwell family.)

I learned a lot from John. And I never forgot that my relationship with him wouldn't have come to be if he hadn't embraced my vision, a vision so many others had found so easy to dismiss. The lesson to me was clear: Trust your passion, identify your dreams, and find the courage to share them with others, no matter how many times they call you a fool. If your vision has merit, no matter how impossible it may seem, someone will recognize it and help you make it come true. That's the practical power of a well-founded dream. Furthermore, experience has taught me that when one dream comes true, others soon follow. At Manchester Bidwell, we've seen that happen so often we've come to depend on it.

For example, one day after the new center was up and running, I received a visit from Dr. Peter Benzing, a chemist from Bayer, another locally based company. Peter, an aficionado of Frank Lloyd Wright, loved the form and design of the building and the spirit he sensed inside of it. After an extended tour of the facility, Peter and I sat down. "We hear you've been training food technicians for Heinz," he said. "We need chemical technicians at Bayer. We'd like to work with you on creating a program that would give us the kind of employees we're looking for."

I was impressed with Peter's faith in us. I knew from plain experience that many people in positions of power had low opinions of the capabilities of poor black people. It would be hard to convince most people that inner-city folks, many of whom didn't have high school diplomas, some of whom could barely read, could be taught the complex math they'd need to perform the highly technical jobs Peter had in mind. But Peter believed it was possible, and he trusted us to do it because he trusted our mission and our vision, and recognized its power.

Out of that meeting with Peter, and with the support of Bayer executives Dick White and Lee Noble, grew our highly successful chem tech program, which is still going strong today, funneling countless students every year into good jobs at Bayer, Mylan Labs, and other chemical companies in the Pittsburgh region. Impressed by the program's success, the chairman of Thrift Drugs, then the largest drug-distribution system in the city, sought out a partnership with us that resulted in the creation of our pharmacy tech program. In similar fashion, we later teamed up with local hospitals to form our medical coding program, which helps students master the arcane codes and practices of hospital billing. There would be other partnerships, as well, in the years ahead.

At the old Bidwell Training Center, it was sometimes hard to get corporate heavyweights to take my calls. At the new center, they sensed something powerful and new, and they wanted to be part of it. All traces of the old center and its sorry culture were gone. Manchester Bidwell wasn't a building trades school anymore, going through the motions of preparing students for jobs they'd be lucky to land. Instead, we were training highly skilled, well-paid workers and placing the great majority of them in dignified, substantial jobs. We had done what we set out to do—put poor black folks at the cutting edge of emerging opportunities. By doing that we had added something new to the whole conversation about poverty and race. Society has always seen poor folks as a social burden, people in need of charity and assistance. But we showed the poor to be people of unlimited potential, assets to the community and valued employees to the companies that hired them. When corporations supported us now, it wasn't out of social obligation. It was because our programs worked—for the community and for their own bottom lines. We had found a point where the interests of capitalists and the interests of inner-city folks intersected. We had turned conventional attitudes about the poor upside down.

As Bidwell flourished at the new center, the Manchester Craftsmen's Guild, aimed at high school kids, also thrived under the same roof. The ceramics program moved into a big and beautiful studio, with soaring ceilings and tall windows that bathed the rooms in daylight. The photo program got bright new classrooms and darkrooms fitted out with professional-caliber gear. As years passed, we added a digital arts curriculum and a program in the visual arts. We hired topflight instructors, most of them established professionals in their fields, and did everything we could to establish an atmosphere of creative ambition and academic achievement of the kind that you'd find at the best private art academies.

As word of our success and our mission got around, we found that big-name artists were eager to conduct workshops at our school— people like world-famous ceramics artists Val Cushing and Don Reitz, legendary photographer Gordon Parks, and acclaimed photojournalist Ben Fernandez—giving our kids the priceless experience of working side by side with established masters. The quality of our programs gave us the ability to reach beyond Manchester, and soon we were drawing students from poor and working-class white neighborhoods as well as predominantly black sections of town. Today, we have almost as many whites as African-Americans in our student body. For me, that kind of wide acceptance, along with the ease and even enthusiasm with which these groups interact at the school, is one of the most powerful validations of what we have accomplished. But there are so many ways to gauge our success.

The power of the Manchester Bidwell philosophy can be measured in the number of public school kids we send on to higher education, the high percentage of Bidwell graduates we place in jobs, the ever-deepening levels of support we're receiving from all segments of society, and in all the honors and recognition we've received, including that genius award I told you about. But it wasn't genius that built this place, or strategy, or any brilliant intention. Manchester Bidwell grew organically out of my experience and my imagination. It was the unlikely, unforeseen, and, I would argue, inevitable result of my desperate pursuit of a dream. All my life I'd been chasing after an intuition of what my life could be. I glimpsed it in the light at Frank Lloyd Wright's Fallingwater. I sensed it in that sunny autumn afternoon in Ligonier. I bathed in it on sun-streaked afternoons at the Guild on Buena Vista Street, where kids were working at the wheels and the place was filled with light and intense energy. But I discovered it in its most potent form in Frank Ross's classroom. Frank's classroom was a place where anything, and everything, seemed to be possible. Hope had a home there. It was a place where it was easy to imagine the extraordinary. I spent most of my life longing to find another place like that, and, through a series of unpredictable events, that longing led me to build one. Manchester Bidwell is nothing more than an elaboration, an expansion, and a living celebration of the magical classroom at Oliver High that Frank Ross created for me. Mr. Ross showed me, and others, that any dream was within our reach. And now he's teaching that same lesson, through me, to hundreds of people every year. I see so many desperate lives that are being changed for the better, and I know that those changes will ripple down through other generations to touch thousands of other lives. How can I doubt the wisdom of the lesson Frank taught me? When I walk down the halls of my building, a building that was built with nothing but trust in a dream, how can I—how can anyone—believe that any dream is beyond their reach?

CHAPTER FIVE

The Secret to Success

One of the first jazz masters to appear on the stage of our music hall was the legendary trumpet player Dizzy Gillespie. When he walked through the doors and looked around, his face lit up with that famous bug-eyed smile. "What *is* this place?" he asked me.

"This is my idea of a school," I told him. Then I took him on a tour. I showed him the ceramics studio, where kids from the street were bent over potter's wheels, lost in the creative struggle to shape lumps of clay into something beautiful. In our chem tech classrooms he saw formerly homeless people unraveling the mystery of complex logarithmic equations, and in the kitchen he watched single mothers and laid-off factory workers put the finishing touches on delicate pastries and pull golden-brown soufflés from the big commercial ovens. I introduced him to students and teachers alike. "This is Dizzy Gillespie," I said, "one of the greatest jazz musicians ever."

After one of those introductions, Dizzy smiled at me and said, "You know, you're a hell of a jazz musician yourself."

Dizzy's comment threw me. "Musician?" I chuckled. "I don't even play an instrument."

Dizzy raised his eyebrows, as if to say, *Don't you think I know a jazz tune when I see one?* Then he thumped my chest with his finger and said, "This *place* is your instrument, man, and everything that happens here is your song."

It was the kind of compliment that takes your breath away, and I nodded humbly, thinking I knew what Dizzy meant. I thought he was making a casual, poetic comment on the improvisational nature of the place, the way the rhythms and harmonies of everything happening here—the flowers, the science, the cooking, the clay—wove together into an integrated, swinging whole that was somehow more than the sum of its eclectic parts. What true jazzman wouldn't notice that? And what greater validation could I ask for than to be commended for it by someone of Dizzy's stature?

But in the twenty-odd years since we started our jazz program, I've had the privilege of spending time with dozens of great jazz artists—most of the premier players on the planet have graced our stage—and as I understood more and more clearly what the music meant to them, I realized what Dizzy was really trying to say: that nobody could have *planned* a place like this. It had to rise up, had to be *conjured* up, as a natural, almost inevitable expression of someone's desperate search for meaning and purpose. Without knowing a thing about me, Dizzy could see how my whole life led up to this place, how my restless quest to live a life that mattered had forced me to mine a lifetime of emotional experience, make sense of it, draw a vision from it, then find the knowledge, skill, partnerships, and perseverance I needed to make that vision real. It's something everyone who has a passion for living does—whether they are a painter, a father, a musician, or an athlete. Dizzy knew all about that process. He'd spent a lifetime doing it. And it was that process he called "jazz." It took me years to realize that when Dizzy said that to me all those years ago, he wasn't just paying me a compliment. He was offering me, offering all of us, a metaphor that helped me make sense of my own peculiar journey through this world.

We all go on unlikely journeys in our lives. As a young man in Manchester, I couldn't have plotted—I couldn't have *imagined*—the unlikely path that carried me to the life I lead today. I never pursued strategic goals or chased after some conventional idea of success. Instead, I moved intuitively from opportunity to opportunity, seeking out one meaningful experience after another, weaving a career out of modest possibilities, new friendships, hunches, lucky breaks, and whatever knowledge and skill I could gather along the way. I think all of our lives are like that to a certain extent. Chance occurrences and unforeseen opportunities play a huge role in all of our lives. I had no master life plan, no grand strategic vision that led me to build Manchester Bidwell. I only followed the longing in my heart and did what I could with the cards that were dealt me. And somehow, that path led me to the very place I wanted and needed to go. When Dizzy told me I was a jazz musician, he made me understand that I had lived my life as a long and winding jazz improvisation. Even though I never played a note of music in my life, I think I know what jazz performers feel. They don't play from a formula or from any conventional wisdom; they take risks, they stretch, they explore, always looking for new opportunities, and always trusting their talents and their instincts to bring them home. I believe that life demands the same ability to trust and improvise. We all need to have the vision and flexibility to react, recover, and keep moving forward every time life hits a snag or throws us an unexpected curve. It is the way we respond to these improvisational demands, embrace them, and use them to further our lives that defines us as musicians in touch with the melodies and harmonies of life.

When a jazz artist launches on a solo, he takes a frightening leap of faith. Every note, every phrase, every bit of color and texture he or she brings to the music is a risk that could backfire and make the player look like a fool. He could play himself into a corner. Worse, he could play himself out and find he had nothing to say. It's a terrifying kind of free fall, but it's the only reason any real musician plays jazz—to find something new in the music, to find something new in himself. And that is true in every one of our lives. The choices we make are incredibly risky. They could lead to surprising and sometimes disastrous consequences. But when we risk ourselves, our time, our careers for what we believe, we can accomplish things we never imagined. We can achieve the impossible. The goal is to plumb the deepest longings of our hearts—for freedom, for solace, for joy, to help others—then try to capture those feelings in a song that adds meaning to our lives and maybe, if we're lucky, some hope and harmony to the world. That's what Dizzy saw at Manchester Bidwell, and that's why he said the place was my song.

Frank Ross, who turned me on to jazz, would have loved to hear that. Frank always had jazz playing in his classroom, and he made sure I appreciated the music, too. He loaned me his favorite albums—Nancy Wilson, Stan Getz, Wes Montgomery, Carmen McRae, Antonio Carlos Jobim—and I would stay up until the early hours listening to them, becoming so lost in the music that the whole world would fade away. The streets of the ghetto outside my door would vanish, and my heart would be filled with sweet longing to do something with my life that would be as hip and true and healing and swinging as the music that was filling up my soul. That longing has always been a guiding light; I trust it to show me the way. Jazz and the sentiments behind it have been a powerful beacon that helped keep my intentions, ambitions, and actions in alignment with the things that mattered most to me. I'm convinced by the experience of a lifetime, by the success of our students, and by so many successful people I admire that the intelligent, responsible pursuit of things that really matter—to the spirit, to the soul—is the best and most reliable path to genuine success in the world. Jazz helped me discover the meaning in my heart, and it gave me the language I needed to express it. By understanding jazz, I understood the power of passion as a motivational fuel. Jazz gave me a style for forging partnerships and personal connections. It taught me how to weather hard times, how to use my strengths, my weaknesses, to my best advantage. But mostly, jazz gave me moments of exhilaration that showed me exactly how a life should *feel*. Whatever success I've enjoyed has come as a direct result of my tireless pursuit of those moments—moments of joy and affirmation, when your values, talents, dreams, and skills fall into alignment and everything you care about just starts to *swing*.

For me, jazz is one of the most powerful metaphors I've ever found for living an extraordinary life, but that won't mean much to you unless you understand very clearly how I define the term. Jazz isn't just the music, it's the feeling the music gives you. That feeling is the result of an ability to recognize potential in simple things and ordinary situations, then, through improvisation, conviction, and skill, turn that potential into something remarkable. (A gifted jazz musician, for example, can make a complex masterpiece out of a tune as simple as "Mary Had a Little Lamb.") Jazz is a state of mind in which possibilities for innovation and discovery are revealed to you, and you are able to tap into deep reserves of commitment and passion. All my life, music has been a gateway to these insights, but it is certainly not the only one. I've experienced moments like these while doing creative things—working in my garden or doing my pottery—but I've also experienced this kind of jazz in the professional arena when giving my speech to an especially receptive audience, for example, or watching some new vision for my school take shape. Jazz for me is a state of mind in which I'm reconnected, with conviction and clarity, to the things that matter most to me. It is a bottomless source of energy and inspiration that reminds me, in simple human terms, why I need to do what I do, and gives me the will and the stamina to keep doing it, despite setbacks and obstacles. You don't have to love jazz music to tap into that state of mind. It doesn't matter if you never listened to a jazz record in your life. Like I said, the music is just a gateway. Your gateway might be kids, or cooking, or golf, or church, or running an organization that makes a difference in the lives of your employees and your customers and maybe does some good for the world. Jazz is the thing that centers you and quiets your mind, and if we pay attention it will open the door to the wisdom we all carry inside us, the wisdom that tells us what matters, what's possible, and what our lives should be.

In the 1930s, a young saxophone player from Kansas City showed up on the stages of the best jazz clubs in New York, playing with such virtuosity that even the best jazz artists of the day could only shake their heads in awe. His name was Charlie Parker, and he became an overnight phenomenon. Now, I have to be honest; I'm no fan of Charlie Parker the man. In many ways he was a mean, sometimes treacherous person, and his self-destructive tendencies and reckless abuse of drugs and alcohol eventually killed him at the age of thirty-four. But despite the mess he made of his personal life, he understood that music was a way of seeing some deeper meaning in the world.

"I kept thinking, there's bound to be something else," he said. "I could hear it, but I couldn't play it."

Parker's frustration was that the vision, the potential, the *meaning* he sensed in the music was beyond his abilities as a musician, as astonishing as those abilities were. He struggled, every time he picked up his saxophone, to deepen his vision, strengthen his technique, and lengthen the reach of his talent. The act of playing his horn became a desperate search for the elusive music he could hear only in his heart. After months of struggling and failing, Parker's search was finally rewarded.

As the story goes, Parker was playing at a New York chili house one night, soloing on a notoriously difficult tune called "Cherokee," when the music opened up to him in a whole new way. It would take a jazz scholar to explain precisely what Parker discovered that night, but in simplest terms, Charlie found a new way to draw melody lines from the chords other band members were playing. The effect of this discovery was huge, because it freed Parker from the traditional structures of rhythm and harmony that had shaped jazz music, and limited jazz soloists, since the earliest days of the art.

Now Parker was free to unleash his fierce talent, steering his dazzling solos in any direction he wanted. He carved out melody lines that looped, dove, circled, and soared so intricately and with such blinding speed that some of his fans would play his 45 rpm records at 33 rpm just to hear what the guy was doing. But no matter how far and how wildly he strayed from the melody, Parker could still resolve his solos in the rhythms and harmonies of the song. Before that night at the chili house, Parker was a work in progress. After his revelation, he became a true genius, an artist whose music fundamentally changed the nature of jazz. Jazz historians could write volumes on the impact of Parker's epiphany, but for Parker himself, the effect of the revelation was a relatively simple matter.

"I could play the things I'd been hearing," he said. "I came alive."

I'm convinced that the moment of insight Charlie Parker had at the chili house is the moment all true jazz artists, all people who search for meaning in their lives, strive for. They dig down past compromise, past imitation, past all the conventional wisdom about what's important or true. For them, every performance, each day, is a chance to discover new depth, new range, new tone, new phrasing. These individuals reach, they stretch, and they grow. For them, the very act of living is an opportunity to find new and richer meaning in the music, in what they do. They don't strive this way to become virtuosos. On the contrary, they become virtuosos in order to express the music they hear in their hearts.

But even though it was jazz music and jazz musicians who gave me the language to grasp this, musicians and music lovers have no monopoly on this state of mind. One of the finest pieces of "jazz" I ever saw, in fact, was produced by an elderly woman who lived on our street when I was a young kid. She lived in one of the modest but well-kept row houses that characterized the neighborhood at the time. Every morning she was out on the sidewalk with a bucket of steaming water and a scrub brush, scouring the concrete stoop at her front door. She was always sweeping her sidewalk, picking up litter from the curb, tending the flowers in the flower boxes that hung at her windows. When Manchester started its slow decline, and the neighborhood deteriorated around her, she never stopped sweeping that concrete, never stopped scrubbing that stoop. She never let what was happening in the neighborhood define her. "This is *my* home," she was telling us. "This is *my* life. I'm not going to let this nonsense touch me. . . ." That was a woman with a vision for how her world should operate, a woman who knew what it meant to be alive, and despite all the odds stacked against her, she found a way to take her spirit, her determination, her strength, and the slim options that were available to her and weave them together into a piece of the world that belonged to her.

For me, "jazz" is essentially a word that describes the discovery of something true and empowering; it puts me in touch with feelings, insights, possibilities, and passions I might not otherwise have found. One of the earliest examples of the power of jazz in my life happened in Mr. Ross's classroom, when I was first learning to work with clay. In those days, it was a thrill just to get a piece to stand up on the potter's wheel, be fairly symmetrical, and come out of the kiln in one piece. But as I developed my technique, I wanted something more; I wanted to create pots that were genuinely beautiful. And that presented a problem: What should those beautiful pots look like? I had a vague intuition of what I wanted my pots to be, but I couldn't visualize that. I didn't know how to capture it in clay. Mr. Ross gave me books full of photographs of pieces made by master ceramics artists. I studied them for inspiration and produced my own variations of the ones I liked the best, but they didn't give me the feeling I was after. I also made some pots based on sheer imagination, but although they were well-shaped and technically sound, their shapes were not satisfying. The process was random and arbitrary, and ultimately frustrating—I could make a decent pot, I just couldn't make it mine.

Then, one morning while I was working at the wheel, Mr. Ross put some jazz on the stereo. He always played jazz during class, but this morning the music seemed to speak to me more clearly than ever before. It was Stan Getz playing Brazilian jazz. I got lost in the sinuous lines of Getz's brilliant saxophone solos, and for a moment I forgot myself and my struggle to shape the clay. I just stood there with my hands on the clay swinging to the music, and as the rhythm got under my skin, I felt the pot moving differently in my hands, as if there was life and intention in the clay. That pot was dancing to the music, man! It was shaping itself. For a moment, it felt like magic, although I knew that whatever was happening was real. The music was opening up my heart and my mind, it was putting me in touch with a feeling, a vision for the clay; it was turning the vision into rhythm and movement that guided my hands, and then I couldn't help but shape a pot that felt the same way.

That was the first pot I created that only *I* could have made. There was nothing random or arbitrary about it. It was a tangible expression of unspoken convictions I had about grace, form, and beauty. I realized that I didn't *choose* how to make that pot, I discovered it by discovering what was alive in me. That was a moment of penetrating clarity. As I experienced more moments like that, in the art room and other areas of my life as well, I began to realize that a life can be shaped out of something more than conventional wisdom or borrowed goals.

A successful life can be built—*must* be built—out of the simple and profound experiences and values that make us feel most human and most alive. Those experiences might involve pottery or art. They may grow out of the impact of a relationship. They may arise from bicycling or football. They may spring from a passion for science and mathematics, for plumbing the unknown. It may come from teaching others.

I STUMBLED ON another kind of jazz as a high school senior when I participated, as a member of Mr. Ross's art class, in that memorable visit to Frank Lloyd Wright's Fallingwater. The startling beauty of that amazing house, rising improbably from rocky ledges in a deep-green forest, stayed with me all my life. Wright was commissioned to build the house in 1936 by Edgar Kaufmann, the wealthy owner of a large Pittsburgh department store, on a pristine parcel of wooded property the Kaufmanns owned in the mountains about seventy miles southeast of Pittsburgh. Kaufmann wanted a rustic summer home situated in such a way that it would provide a view of the lovely waterfall that tumbled down over rocky outcrops on the property. Instead, Wright built an iconoclastically modern structure of glass, steel, and native stone, defined by massive horizontal levels of poured concrete that cantilevered dramatically out from the core of the house and rested on invisible supports. The building seemed to float in the trees. Whatever Kaufmann's reaction to the design of the house, he must have been baffled by where Wright decided to put it. Because instead of choosing a site for the house that would show off the waterfall view to its best advantage, Wright built the house in the one spot where you couldn't see the waterfall at all—directly above the falls, anchored upon the rocky ledges over which the water flowed.

Now, conventional wisdom about building and construction tells us that water is the enemy of houses. But Wright was not afraid to defy that convention, or the conventional expectations of his client, or the warnings of Kaufmann's conventionally minded engineers who were certain that the house's massive cantilevered extensions were destined to tumble down onto the rocks below. Where did Wright find such conviction? Why did he risk disaster? Why would he take the chance of making a fool of himself and offending a powerful client (from whom he would later receive commissions worth what would today equal millions of dollars)?

I think he did those things for the same reason a jazz musician turns a party song into a reflective ode to life, or turns a composition upside down by playing an A-minor chord when anyone who knows anything about music would expect him to play a B-flat major. Wright did it because all his experience, all his expertise, his sense of order and meaning and everything he knew about truth and beauty, told him that the only place for that house was right at the top of that waterfall. He followed the song in his heart, used concrete and steel the way a jazz musician uses harmony and rhythm. He forgot about how things are *supposed* to be and instead just trusted his vision. He made the impossible possible, and in the process he produced what is widely considered one of the most beautiful houses on the planet.

Now, I don't know if Frank Lloyd Wright ever heard a jazz tune in his life. But the cat knew jazz—the jazz that is more than music, in which your heart is open, your vision clear, and all your passion, talent, values, and dreams are aligned to accomplish the things that matter to you the most. This is the way to build an extraordinary house, play an extraordinary tune, live an extraordinary life. It's the way I built my center. That's the kind of jazz I'm talking about, jazz as a gateway to authentic experience, as a lens that gives you the clarity of vision you need to realize what it means to be alive. Dizzy said Manchester Bidwell was my song. We all have that kind of song in our hearts, a song that tells us who we are and what we genuinely want from life. It may play very softly, and it easily gets lost in the random clamor of everyday living, but if you listen, if you develop an ear for it, you'll hear it everywhere and your life will never look the same.

THERE'S A SCENE in *Man's Search for Meaning*, Viktor Frankl's powerful memoir of life in the Nazi death camps, that for me perfectly captures what life is all about with breathtaking clarity. Frankl was a psychiatrist who spent three years as a prisoner at Auschwitz and other concentration camps. He lost his parents, his brother, and his pregnant wife in the Holocaust. The moment he describes below comes at the end of another day of brutal and dehumanizing captivity.

One evening, when we were already resting on the floor of our hut, dead tired, soup bowls in hand, a fellow prisoner rushed in and asked us to run out to the assembly grounds and see the wonderful sunset. Outside we saw sinister clouds glowing in the west and the whole sky alive with clouds of ever-changing shapes and colors, from steel blue to blood red. The desolate gray mud huts provided a sharp contrast, while the puddles on the muddy ground reflected the glowing sky. . . .

Frankl says they watched in silence for several minutes, stunned by this reminder that there was beauty in the world. These were men who had lost their families, lost their hope, had had every shred of dignity taken away from them. They were dressed in rags; some of them were not much more than skin and bones. But their hearts still knew the value of beauty. In that moment, those men were free, and in the face of all that beauty they rediscovered what it meant to feel alive in the fullest sense of the word.

All of us have moments like this, moments of revelation and insight, epiphanies that seem to stop time, when we remember who we are and what we want our lives to be. In my experience, these moments tend to be brief and elusive. The pressures and distractions of our everyday concerns quickly overtake them. "Practical" considerations call our attention to other things; we lose touch with these moments and spend our days sleepwalking, thinking about the tasks and to-do lists of our lives, mistakenly assuming they are the same thing as life itself. We need to look in the mirror once in a while and remind ourselves of the truth: That we really are alive, man! Our life is happening *now*! It's like we're dreaming and we have all the time in the world. I am convinced that you cannot hope to live a great life, a life that achieves your fullest potential, until you wake up to the fact that life is tangible, immediate, and precious. If we don't embrace the reality that our life *is what is taking place in this moment,* our life will never be entirely our own. It will always be something we chase after. And that chase will seem like the most natural thing in the world.

It has always struck me as odd that we take so naturally to metaphors that describe life as a process of forward motion. You hear it all the time. We talk about a "ladder to success." When someone shows promise, we say, "He's going places." When someone hits it big, winning an executive position or a recording contract or an endowed chair at a prestigious university, it seems natural to say, "She has arrived." The logic of these clichés seems so compelling and self-evident that we rarely think to question it. But we should. Because these phrases are more than harmless figures of speech. In fact, they bear a powerful message that shapes our ambitions and, I believe, limits our potential for leading extraordinary lives. They tell us that life is a specific path that must be followed—that whatever joy, fulfillment, and affirmation you long for in your life lie off in some vague and distant future. In other words, that the life you dream of living is somewhere other than *right here* and *right now*. It's something external, something that exists out there somewhere along one path or another. You must choose your path, then chase after it and find a place for yourself in it, like a commuter racing for one of a few good seats on the bus or train.

On the surface, it all seems to make perfect sense, but a moment of clear reflection reveals the flimsiness of that vision. There are no roads that lead us to happiness and no ladders waiting to lead us up to success. An authentic life is not something we pursue, it's something that must be created out of the passion and values that matter to us each and every day. "Now" is the only solid reality you can count on. Now is when you build a future that matters. Jazz, my kind of jazz, won't let you forget that; it won't let you settle for a life built on conventional standards of achievement or someone else's definition of success. It shows you how to develop the strengths, values, vision, and commitment you need to make your most personal dreams come true. It teaches you how to sing the song of your life, and to build a life that is genuinely and successfully your own.

That's what we teach at Manchester Bidwell. We aren't simply equipping our students with some artistic training or specific job skills, we're teaching them the art of living; we're giving them rich and transforming experiences that give them a visceral understanding of how a good human life should *feel*. After all, why should some troubled and aimless kids buy your plan for their future when they've had no experiences that tell them such a future is worth striving for? So we don't give them warmed-over War on Poverty rhetoric, or lectures on responsibility and self-esteem. Instead, we invite them into a hip, sunlit building. We surround them with fresh flowers, creative energy, and beautiful things. We introduce them to famous artists and jazz musicians. We feed them gourmet food.

We give them something to believe in, something to be part of, something that not only promises them a future but enriches the quality of their lives *right here* and *right now*. We want them to buy a *concept*—that a meaningful life is already within their reach—and to get them to buy it we do everything we can to give them a sense of what it might feel like to live a life that *swings*. We all respond more powerfully to things that can change our life *today*. Once they get a taste of that kind of life, and the purpose, pride, and meaning that it brings, they want more of it. That's when their hearts open up to new possibilities and they begin to explore their own potential, disclosing new talents and building on their strengths, listening for the song they were always meant to sing.

And that's the essence of innovation as it's practiced at Manchester Bidwell. But if you think that a good life built on trust and meaningful experience is useful only to the poor, you've missed the point. I'm convinced that no genuine success occurs except as a natural expression of the human heart's search for meaning. Yes, there are plenty of "successful" people who make a lot of money or have achieved high corporate positions, who run organizations or have won elective office, who are clueless when it comes to understanding what life is all about. The fact is, that kind of success is only half of the equation. Our drive for titles and money is too often based on a desperate need to prove ourselves to others, rather than the passion to live a life in a way that draws on our true values and talents, enlarges our spirits, and allows us to be who we need to be to live rich, satisfying lives.

Real success, genuine success, can't be chosen and chased down. You assemble it, moment by moment, out of the dreams you choose to follow and the values and passions you share. It's not something you have a choice in—it's a process that occurs, whether we pay attention or not. When we focus on anything other than the things that have real meaning in our life, our life becomes shaped by the random circumstances of the world around us. Even the most materialistically oriented individuals expect, on some level, that the wealth, privilege, and power they achieve will make them happy. But it doesn't work that way. If it did, Hollywood celebrities wouldn't spend so much time in divorce court, rehab, and jail, and fewer lottery winners would see their lives turn into train wrecks after cashing in their tickets. Trying to find meaning in material success is a losing game. I know CEOs making $15 million a year who feel restless and slighted because they know some other CEO is making more. Money and power alone can never make them happy. Believe me, the hunger for material success is an addiction, just like booze or drugs. It burns up your time and energy, drains the humanity from your life, and leaves you wanting more.

Meaning is not something you can add to your life in limited amounts, or defer to a time in your life after you've "made it." Meaning *is* your life, it's who you are. It's all you'll ever have, and in my experience it's the only practical foundation for a life worth living. No genuine success—in your personal *and* professional life—is possible until you trust the power of the values and experiences that matter to you most.

A FEW YEARS AGO, I was interviewed as part of a study intended to isolate the defining qualities of "enduringly successful people." The researchers asked me to define my view of success. I told them pretty much what I'm telling you—that true fulfillment isn't about chasing some narrow definition of achievement or wealth, it's about trusting the value of your passions and principles and using them as a base to build a life. "Play out your dream," I told them. "There is no second chance. You either choose to impact your environment or your environment will define you."

The results of that study, which involved more than two hundred people, were eventually published in a book titled *Success Built to Last,* by Jerry Porras, Stewart Emery, and Mark Thompson. When the book came out, I was surprised, and humbled, to see whose company I was in—everyone from Jack Welch to the Dalai Lama, from Warren Buffett to Yo-Yo Ma. Virtually all the respondents, whether they were artists like Maya Angelou, political leaders like Newt Gingrich and Madeleine Albright, musicians and cultural rabble-rousers like U2's Bono, or humanitarians like Jimmy Carter and Nelson Mandela, held strong convictions about the nature of success. To a person, these extraordinary individuals said meaning was a more important factor in their success than brains, talent, competitiveness, or career savvy. In the words of the authors:

> Success in the long run has less to do with finding the best idea, organizational structure, or business model for an enterprise, than with discovering what matters to us as individuals. . . . For the most part, extraordinary people, teams, and organizations are simply ordinary people doing extraordinary things that matter to them.

One of the folks who participated in the study is Muhammad Yunus, founder of the Grameen Bank Project and winner of the Nobel Peace Prize. As a young man, Yunus had a passion for economics and education, which helped him earn a Fulbright scholarship and a Ph.D., and eventually land a position as a professor of economics in the United States. When he was thirty-two years old, Yunus returned to his home in Bangladesh and took a position as a government economist. He was bored but comfortable. Then, in 1974, the country was ravaged by floods that killed more than one and a half million people—more than ten times the number who perished in the 2004 tsunami. Bangladesh, one of the world's poorest countries, struggled to right itself. Yunus saw families living on the edge of starvation. Some of them tried to create businesses that made use of their skills—weaving cloth, making household goods, building simple pieces of furniture—but after paying off the local brokers and bosses, there was barely enough money left over to feed themselves and their families.

Yunus realized that it wouldn't take much money for these people to free themselves from the burden of those brokers and bosses, so he began to make small, unsecured loans to poor villagers, asking for no collateral or credit history. The amounts of the loans were minuscule—sometimes less than a dollar and never more than $100—but those small amounts allowed the villagers to establish small businesses, sell the things they made, and lift themselves out of grinding poverty. To date, Grameen Bank has invested more than $5 billion to help poor people in Bangladesh, and the "micro-lending" movement he started has spread all over the world.

Yunus's hope was "to turn begging bowls into cash boxes." Ed Penhoet, another person profiled in the book, vowed to find a way to bring new cancer cures to the market after watching his favorite uncle die from cancer. That desire led him to a career as a biochemist, and eventually he became cofounder of Chiron, a $1.9-billion biotech innovator. But genuine success is not always motivated by altruistic intentions alone; sometimes it's enough to truly believe that you have a better way to get things done. Jeff Bezos founded Amazon.com out of a belief that he could revolutionize retail markets. His faith in the worthiness of his concept was more powerful than any shallow drive to get rich quick, and so, while other Internet founders were cashing out and getting rich, Bezos made it clear that he was on board for the long haul. He was after something more important, and more satisfying, than money. He wanted to make a difference. From my point of view, what links these three men together, what links all the truly successful people I've ever known, is the fact that they weren't trying to achieve success by any arbitrary measure of wealth, fame, or power. They were simply trying to build organizations, and lives, that mattered to them as human beings. All of them faced long odds but refused to let their dreams perish or die. They didn't ask themselves if their dreams were practical or even possible. They didn't allow themselves to be boxed in by conventional thinking. They followed their hearts, and despite huge obstacles and a thousand sound, practical reasons to give up along the way, they found the strength, faith, resourcefulness, and creativity to make their dreams come true.

That's what I call making the impossible possible, and authentically successful people do it every day of their lives. Everything I've accomplished, from that first piece of pottery to the creation of the Manchester Bidwell Center, has come as the result of trusting the value of things that moved me, touched me, opened my spirit, and added joy or satisfaction to my life. I never had a career strategy; I never created a road map for my life. I had only a sense for how my life should feel. That was my beacon. I didn't build Manchester Bidwell to advance my career. I didn't build it to help poor folks, although the knowledge that it would was a great motivator. I built it because I *had* to build it to be the person I needed to be. I needed to shape the world around me to match the way I wanted my life to feel. The center is an organic, artistic, necessary expression of my long struggle to be me.

That struggle not only propelled me to build the Manchester Bidwell Center, it gave me the philosophy that makes the place work. At the Manchester Craftsmen's Guild, we don't teach students to become artists—we give them experiences that open their minds to the possibility of a fuller, richer life. At the Bidwell Training Center, we don't put folks on the road to success—we teach them the skills and values that a successful life is made of. Many of our students come in feeling that a better life is so far beyond their grasp that it isn't worth reaching for. They feel the road to happiness doesn't run through their neighborhood. We want them to look beyond the options life has offered them and focus on something real, tangible, something they created: the thrill of making a graceful pot, the satisfaction of baking a perfect soufflé, the wonder of raising a prizewinning orchid, or the sense of accomplishment and empowerment you feel when you crack the code of a complex mathematical equation. Those kinds of learning experiences offer our students the first glimpse of what a good life might feel like. That's the clarity we're after, that's the root of making the impossible possible. It's also the root of greatness. I saw it in all my heroes: Martin Luther King Jr., who saw the outrageous possibility of turning back centuries of hatred with dignity and nonviolence; Frank Lloyd Wright, who saw the possibility of building what would become a landmark house on top of a waterfall; and Fred Rogers, one of the most inspiring human beings I've ever known, who saw the possibility of making the world a better place by helping to nurture kinder, happier kids.

I first met Fred when I was running the original Manchester Craftsmen's Guild in the row house on Buena Vista Street. Fred's show, *Mr. Rogers' Neighborhood,* was produced at WQED-TV in Pittsburgh. Fred had heard about the work we were doing with neighborhood kids, so he brought a film crew over and we shot an episode featuring me showing Fred how to throw a pot. It was the start of a friendship that lasted until Fred died. Fred was as gentle and as genuine in person as he was on TV, but behind the childlike innocence he was famous for was an unquestioned conviction about what mattered in his life. Fred was driven to protect and promote the dignity and worth of every child, and that passion made him one of the strongest, most effective advocates I ever knew. Comedians loved making fun of Fred's mild-mannered demeanor, but if you knew Fred Rogers, you knew the truth—he was gentle, but he wasn't meek.

In 1961, the whole nation saw Fred's qualities when he squared off with congressional hawks who wanted to cut $20 million in proposed funding for public broadcasting to finance the Vietnam War. For several days, PBS executives had testified before a congressional committee, chaired by the tough Democratic senator John Pastore. Pastore, no fan of PBS, had grilled the execs harshly, and by the time Fred got his chance to address the committee at the end of the hearings it seemed like any hopes of staving off the budget cuts had disappeared. As Fred took his seat at the microphone, there was an edge of tension and hostility in the room. Fred spoke with the childlike lilt he was famous for, and at first Pastore, who didn't know Fred's show, seemed amused that the hardball budget debate was now going to focus on the testimony of a guy who made his living with puppets and children's songs.

"I give an expression of care to each child to help him realize that he is unique," Fred said. "I end the program by saying, 'You've made this day special by just your being you. There's no person like you, and I like you just the way you are.' And I feel that if we in public television can only make it clear that feelings are mentionable and manageable, we will have done a great service."

Fred talked for several minutes about kindness and dignity and society's responsibility to raise healthy, happy kids. Pastore's face was impassive as Fred finished. He seemed moved, not only by Fred's words but also by the weight of his sincerity. He blinked a few times, then lifted his hand and let it drop to the table.

"That's wonderful," he said quietly. "Just wonderful."

He took a deep breath, glanced up and down the dais.

"Well," he said at last. "It looks like you got your $20 million."

The room erupted into applause. Fred just smiled and nodded.

Now, that's what I call jazz, man. That's what I call jazz.

WHEN FRED ROGERS started his show at WQED in Pittsburgh, educational television was still in its infancy. His budget was $30 per show. All he had were some crude props, some puppets he'd made himself, and the unshakable certainty that he had a message the world needed to hear. From those humble origins he rose to become a national treasure whose pursuit of his vision of children's programming had an immeasurable impact on millions of lives. But here's the thing about Fred: If he had never become famous, if he had never gotten on TV, he would have worked just as hard to spread his message, in church basements, grade school auditoriums, and anywhere else they would have him. He never set out to change the world. He only did what he needed to do to be who he was. And I can't imagine leading a more meaningful life. Few of us can hope to have the impact Fred did, but that's not the point. The lesson is that the first step in living a great life is to live a worthwhile life, and that's something each one of us can do. It's something we must do if we want our lives to matter and to make a difference. What Fred did before Congress, what he did every day of his life, is a powerful example of a guy who knew his own song and spent his lifetime singing it.

Sometimes, the hardest thing about living an exceptional life is realizing what it means, in simplest and most essential terms, to be alive. Just waking up to the fact that you are alive—that each day and each moment you're on the planet gives you a once-in-a-lifetime chance to build the future you dream of—can be an impossibly elusive concept to grasp. We get sucked into the daily grind: Days, weeks, and months slip by; years come and go. Time slips by, whether or not we notice, and too often, moments we'll never have again are lost.

There was a time in my life when I drank too much and I wound up in the hospital, diagnosed with pancreatitis, a debilitating disease of the pancreas. "Your life is about to change," my doctor said. "That is, if you want to keep living much longer. Let's go for a walk." He led me out of my room and into the hall. We walked past a room and the doctor motioned for me to look in. I saw a man on a bed who looked like he was at death's door. In fact, his doctor told me, the man wasn't expected to live much longer. "Pancreatitis," said the doctor. "If you don't stop drinking, that's going to be you." That got my attention. The next day I looked into the room, but the bed was empty and I knew he hadn't gotten better and gone home. He was gone. To me, that was a serious dose of reality, and the shock helped me stop drinking in short order. But it also helped me to create a little exercise I use whenever I lose track of what's important: I imagine myself in that guy's shoes, at the end of my life, with only minutes to live. Then, somehow, I am offered one more day of life to use any way I please.

What would you do if you got such a chance on your deathbed? How would you spend that precious day? Well, now is the time to decide, because that day is today and every day you will ever have. The truth is, your days are numbered. It's a grim and sobering thought, but it's also the essence of clarity, because as the notion of death becomes real, your sense of being alive automatically becomes vividly enhanced. Viktor Frankl's experiences in the death camps taught him the preciousness of life and forced him to confront troubling questions about what a good life is made of. We all want to be happy, he says, but happiness can't be planned. You need a reason to be happy, and once that reason is in place, he says, "happiness ensues."

The same is true of living a satisfying life. Such success can't be pursued; you must have a reason to live a satisfying life, and that reason, Frankl says, is *meaning*.

The sand in the hourglass flows only one way. Don't waste precious time chasing someone else's definition of success. Live your life with purpose *now*. Look for the things that inspire you, trouble you, make you feel most alive, and trust in those things to shape your future. They will give you all your heart could ever wish for.

CHAPTER SIX

Impossibility Thinking

One morning about ten years ago, I walked into the office of Jesse Fife, who was, by then, chief operating officer at the Manchester Bidwell Corporation, and set an outrageously beautiful potted flower on his desk.

"That's an orchid," I said.

"I know it's an orchid," he replied with a wary smile, "but why is it on my desk?" Jesse is one of my closest friends. After working with me for more than thirty-five years, no one understands the way my mind works better than Jesse. He knew I wasn't giving him the flower just because I liked him.

"We're going to grow these," I told him.

Jesse gave me a sober stare. "We're going into the orchid business?" he asked.

I turned the flower so he could better appreciate its beauty.

"Where exactly are we going to grow orchids?" he asked.

"In the greenhouse," I said.

"We don't have a greenhouse," Jesse pointed out.

"Not yet," I conceded.

"You're going to build a *greenhouse*?"

"How can I grow orchids in Pittsburgh without a greenhouse?" I replied.

"Do you have any idea how much that will cost?"

I shrugged. "We need a big one," I said. "State of the art."

Jesse nodded and drummed his fingers on his desk.

"Orchids," he said softly. "Why orchids?" But he wasn't speaking to me—he knew my mind was made up. So instead of answering him, I looked at the plant on his desk. "Damn," I said, "that's a beautiful flower."

I GOT MY FIRST ORCHID as a gift from a friend named Keith Kappmeyer, who was then chairman of our board and a former COO of Blue Cross of Western Pennsylvania. I set it on a window ledge in my dining room and saw right away there was magic in that flower. It glowed in the daylight. At night it filled the room with a radiance of its own. The quality of that light, and the complex, mysterious beauty of that flower, did more than *add* beauty to the dining room; it transformed something fundamental in the room's reality, reorganized the energy of that room according to some new principle, some new priority that's impossible to put into words. I didn't try to translate that feeling into rational terms, but I knew in my bones that it was pointing me toward exciting potential. So I followed it the only way I knew how—I decided to raise orchids of my own. Educating myself about orchids became a passion. I subscribed to orchid-lover magazines, I devoured books written by master orchid growers, and I made myself a regular at Phipps Conservatory, Pittsburgh's public botanical gardens, where I picked the brains of every orchid expert they had on staff. With their advice, I set up a modest orchid nursery in my basement. I spent hours down there in the dim light, often in the quiet after midnight, listening to jazz and tending to my seedlings. But no matter how carefully I cared for the plants, my orchids refused to bloom. I experimented with different soils and temperatures, different levels of moisture and light. Nothing worked. Finally, I had to accept the fact that I couldn't create the kind of environment my orchids needed to thrive in my basement. It would have been a natural point to give up on the dream, and giving up might have been the most sensible thing to do. But my trust in the beauty of the orchids, and the intuition that being true to that trust would lead to something good, made it impossible for me to quit. My mind searched restlessly for a solution. *Who grows orchids?* I asked myself. Experts grow orchids. *Where do they grow them?* In big commercial greenhouses. So I knew what I needed to do. And as soon as I reached that conclusion, my greenhouse became real.

I could see it. I could see the rows of long tables covered with orchids in various stages of growth. I knew how it would feel to stand inside it, how the soft light would radiate down from the glass roof; I could hear the sounds of quiet industry as technicians worked at the tables, tending the delicate plants. I even knew how the place would smell.

I didn't know *how* I would make this happen, but as soon as those images became real to me, my mind opened up to the future this dream might offer—the possibility of new opportunities, new relationships, new ways to broaden and deepen the effectiveness of my school. I also considered the obstacles I'd have to overcome to make the dream come true. Once again I'd be stepping way beyond the boundaries of conventional thinking. I would have to drum up money and support for an idea—growing orchids in the ghetto—that a lot of sensible people might think was insane. But I didn't focus on any of those things too clearly. I didn't try to plot a path or map out a specific strategy. I knew from experience that the urge to turn an intuition into a specific goal can drain all the life and potential from the idea. The greenhouse was already a priority for me, and I was already committed to making it happen. But I wasn't going to limit my possibilities by trying to predict too specifically how I was going to get that done. I wanted to leave room for surprises and unexpected opportunities. I simply trusted my love of the flower to show me the way. So I broke the news to Jesse, and with his enthusiasm and strong support, I did what I could to get the ball rolling.

The first step was to draw up plans for the greenhouse and take them to the Pittsburgh offices of Rick Santorum, who was at the time a U.S. senator from Pennsylvania. We showed Santorum's staff members our blueprints and with their help made a formal application for a federal grant to build a commercial-quality greenhouse in Manchester, just a block from the Manchester Bidwell Center. Weeks passed as we waited to hear the results of our application. During that time, I made a business trip to Los Angeles, and while I was there I took a drive to Malibu to visit a large, nationally known orchid nursery I'd read about in one of my horticultural magazines. The manager of the nursery offered to give me a tour, and the moment I stepped into the place I felt like I'd walked into my own dream. The light, the smells, the sounds, the quiet busyness of the workers, the tables covered with gorgeous orchids stretching out in all directions—it was exactly what I had imagined. *This is it!* I told myself. *This is the feeling I'm after.* At that moment, I knew with rock-solid certainty that my greenhouse was going to happen, that I was looking at my future laid out in front of me.

Then my cell phone rang. It was Santorum's office calling to say our application had been denied. They couldn't find a way to make a horticultural facility fit the criteria of any existing federal grant programs. It didn't make sense to the bureaucrats, it seemed, to build a greenhouse in the ghetto. It was a cruel blow to get that news at a moment when my vision seemed so tangible and so near. That night, as I flew back to Pittsburgh, I tried to find a way to keep my dream alive. Maybe I had been too ambitious, I thought. Maybe I should scale back my ambitions, ask for something smaller. It might even be possible to carve out some space in the existing footprint of the Manchester Bidwell building and convert it to function as a greenhouse. Or maybe I should do the sensible thing and give up the dream altogether. It was a restless flight, but somewhere above the heartland, while most of the other passengers slept, I came to grips with the fact that my trust in the magic of orchids was too strong to allow compromise, and by the time the plane touched down at the Pittsburgh airport I knew what I had to do. I wouldn't give up the dream. I wouldn't scale back my vision. Instead, I'd expand the dream and deepen my trust in it; I would come on stronger. I'd go back to Santorum's office and ask for even *more.*

I realized that the first time around, I had been asking for money to help *my* dream come true. I wanted powerful people to see the value of *my* vision. I'd be smarter the next time around. I'd present my vision in a way that made sense to *them.* There was no way the government would fund a greenhouse. But if they wouldn't give me what I wanted, I'd take what they would give. I knew there was money available for economic development—projects that would bring jobs, tax revenue, and physical improvement to neighborhoods like Manchester. I decided to apply for one of those grants to fund the construction of an office building somewhere near the Manchester Bidwell Center. But I didn't want to approach the senator until I could make my strongest case. It took a lot of work and perseverance to reach that point, and my dream spent several years in limbo, but I never gave up. Finally, we got a break when I caught the attention of one of the toughest and most powerful business leaders in town.

Jeff Romoff is CEO of the University of Pittsburgh Medical Center (UPMC), which, under Jeff's leadership, has become the dominant health care provider in the western Pennsylvania region and one of the leading medical centers in the nation. Jeff is a famously take-no-prisoners, no-nonsense, suffer-no-fools kind of guy. I'd been trying to make a connection with him for years, and when I finally convinced him to visit our center, he started the meeting by saying, "Okay, you have twenty minutes. What is it you want me to see?" I didn't ask for money or any other kind of help. Instead, I rushed him through a scaled-down tour of the school. At one point, he saw me glancing at my watch to see how much time I had left. "Relax," he said. "I like what I see here. I'll give you all the time you need." Jeff came to the meeting thinking I was going to ask for a handout. But I never ask for handouts; I just show people what we're up to and leave it up to them to see the benefit of being part of what we're trying to get done. Jeff saw that Manchester Bidwell wasn't doing charity, that we were building lives. He saw that what we do was working, and like a lot of clear-headed people who get to know the place, he wanted to be part of it. But Jeff's attraction to the place was based on something more than pure altruism; he saw a pragmatic reason for UPMC to help us succeed.

"When a kid comes into one of our emergency rooms with a gunshot wound, it can cost as much as $150,000 to treat him," he told me. "I have a vested interest in keeping kids out of trouble. What is it you wanted to talk to me about?"

I told him I wanted to build an office building and I wanted UPMC to be the anchor tenant. It would require him to move part of his billing operation from UPMC's base in the Oakland section of town— a neighborhood of universities, museums, and cultural centers—to the poor, high-crime streets of Manchester. I'm not sure why he agreed, but I'm sure that the chance to build a relationship with Manchester Bidwell was part of it, and in the end he committed to renting out most of the building as office space for UPMC's billing operations.

My next step was to find a building site. There was an ideal parcel of land just down the street from the center. Half of it was owned by the Pittsburgh Urban Renewal Authority, and we were able to acquire it from them on a long-term, deeply discounted lease/purchase deal. The other half belonged to Mellon Bank. With UPMC on board, it wasn't hard to get the bank to take me seriously, and eventually they agreed to donate the land to our cause free of charge, primarily due to the extraordinary leadership of their chairman, Marty McGuinn.

We designed a four-story office building to suit UPMC's needs, and with the help of Pittsburgh architect Lou Astorino (who has built noteworthy structures all over the world, including a recently completed and highly praised private chapel at the Vatican), we made sure that the building would offer the aesthetically refined environment

Manchester Bidwell is known for. When the blueprints were finished, I took them to Santorum's office and rolled them out on a desk.

"UPMC is renting most of the space," I said. "We'll use the rest for classrooms or storage." I pointed out that the new building would bring new jobs and tax revenue into the community. The building itself, and the surrounding grounds, which included a pleasant courtyard, would make a huge aesthetic improvement in the neighborhood.

The staffer nodded in understanding. It all made perfect sense. Then she pointed to a rectangular shape on the blueprint, a footprint for a second structure flanking the main building. "What's this?" she asked.

"Well," I said, "this particular economic development package comes with a state-of-the-art, 40,000-square-foot greenhouse."

She smiled. I smiled. I knew I was going to get the money, and in 2003, almost seven years since I'd first laid that orchid on Jesse's desk, the greenhouse was up and running. We staffed the place with experts who helped us develop a first-rate horticulture program, giving us another way to help Bidwell students start new lives. That program has turned out legions of graduates since the greenhouse opened, helping most of them find good jobs—as designers and installation technicians for landscaping contractors, and in sales and management positions for floral wholesalers or retail flower shops. Some of them have even started landscaping firms of their own. It's a safe bet that few of our horticulture students had ever owned an orchid before they enrolled in the program—some of them had never even seen one—but their potential for growing these demanding plants is clear: Recently, orchids grown by our students have won awards, including Best in Show at an annual symposium of the Western Pennsylvania

Orchid Society. Because of their quality, our flowers are always in high demand. Whole Foods now sells our orchids. So does the large regional supermarket chain Giant Eagle, whose chairman, David Shapira, is a close friend and valued corporate partner, and whose insights about our school are quoted in one of the case studies Harvard Business School did on Manchester Bidwell. You can also find our orchids at smaller floral shops throughout the area. We make some money from that, and our success with growing flowers has led to other uses for the greenhouse. We're growing and selling cucumbers now, and we are looking into new possibilities for raising other hothouse vegetables, including gourmet beefsteak tomatoes.

Tomatoes were nowhere on my radar screen when I first fell in love with that orchid, but I've learned that if you have a worthy dream and you find the guts to trust it, astonishing things can happen. For example, the greenhouse has become a magnet for drawing people and new energy into Manchester Bidwell. All sorts of horticultural societies tour the place, and many of them hold meetings and functions there. Recently, we hosted an organic food convention in the greenhouse that had New Wave Asian chefs, New Age health food gurus, and traditional Amish farmers all rubbing shoulders. I don't know what will come out of all that activity, but it raises the profile of our operations and reaches out to new groups of people in ways that might create exciting new possibilities for the center and our students. Building the greenhouse also solidified our corporate partnerships: Our relationship with Mellon Bank is stronger than ever, and Jeff Romoff and UPMC have become one of our most generous and most trusted supporters. But many of the most meaningful benefits the greenhouse has produced are less tangible and more human. Many of our students have been hardened by the difficulty of their lives. They come to us hiding behind a tough outer shell that protects them, but it also blocks them from trusting in the kinds of positive experiences the human spirit needs to know in order to grow and flourish. That hardness may have served its purpose in the streets, but it doesn't survive for long in the greenhouse. There's something about the care and delicacy required to raise an orchid, something about seeing your efforts blossom, almost magically, into a thing of such delicacy and striking beauty, that has a healing, transforming effect on the human spirit. If you need proof that the human heart is resilient, and that beauty and hope and high expectations can work wonders in even the most difficult lives, I can't imagine a better way to find it than by raising an orchid.

I couldn't have laid out a strategy that would have led to the partnerships that the orchids have made real. I couldn't have mustered the cleverness and foresight to look into the future and see these things as *goals*. But my point is, I didn't have to. All I had to do was trust my intuition that there was something powerful in the beauty of a flower. That freed me from the need to choose, to pursue some distant, abstract goal. Instead, I focused on something more practical and more real—the beauty of the orchid—and my trust in that vision blossomed into more good things than I ever could have imagined.

In 1996, the MacArthur Foundation gave me one of their fellowship awards—often known as "genius" grants—for the kind of thinking that made the greenhouse possible. I don't take the award too literally—my feet are planted way too firmly on the ground here in Manchester to let things like that go to my head. But still, I figure it at least gives me the right to say what I think about the nature of genius itself. The term conjures up some lofty connotations. We use it to describe the immortals of human history—people like Einstein, Beethoven, Michelangelo, and Da Vinci—whose insights and accomplishments have changed the way we see the world. These heroic figures seem to have been born with almost superhuman powers of intellect and imagination, and it's easy to see them as members of a higher order of human being.

But genius is not the same thing as IQ or talent. It's not something you're born with. It's not something you *are*. Genius is something you discover. We all have access to genius. It runs through our lives like a vein of gold. The people we call "geniuses" have found a way to tap this vein and use the power of their own potential to do remarkable things. In Latin, "genius" means "helpful spirit." It's from the same root word that gives us "genie," the magical being in a bottle who makes wishes come true. It's the power of that spirit that amplifies and focuses the lives of the people we call geniuses and enables them to accomplish things that can't be done by talent or intellect alone. What's important for the rest of us to remember is that we all have access to that spirit. And we summon it not by doing what seems most practical, but by trusting what feels most meaningful and most real. Galileo wasn't out to sell a theory; he was only watching the sky, absorbed by the elegance and mystery of the movement of the planets. What he saw had always been there for anyone to see, but he had the clarity and imagination and trust in his observations to see it. Beethoven was trying to give shape to the music that was already real in his head. Michelangelo chipped away at the marble until he discovered the statue he knew was locked inside the stone.

"To see a thing in the seed, that is genius," said Lao-tzu. Few of us have the natural gifts of an Einstein or a Michelangelo, but all of us have the spirit of genius inside us. And we lose touch with it when we turn our mind to the "practical" pursuits of life: setting goals, developing strategies to reach those goals, limiting our options, or allowing others to constrain our notions of what's real and what's important in order to live the kind of life our goals demand.

To reconnect with the spirit of genius requires a different kind of practicality, one that isn't based on conventional ideas of what we *should* believe, or how we should *expect* our lives to be. We need to see past the limitations of conventional wisdom and common sense and develop the clear-eyed, uncompromising practicality of the artist.

In our goal-driven, achievement-based society, artists aren't often held up as paragons of the practical. But true artists are, by nature, profoundly pragmatic beings. They take life as it comes, they trust direct experience more than secondhand wisdom, and they value the importance of things just as they are. "The artist is a receptacle for emotions that come from all over the place," said Picasso, "from the sky, from the earth, from a scrap of paper, from a passing shape, from a spider's web."*

In other words, artists draw inspiration directly from the source. They deal in what is simply and undeniably real. The basic act of artistic creation, in fact, is to see the essential realness of a thing. The better the artist, the deeper he or she sees into that essence. Artists tend to peel away layers of falseness. That is one of the reasons I

---

* Pablo Picasso (1881–1973), Spanish artist. "Conversation avec Picasso," in *Cahiers d'Art*, volume 10, number 10 (1935); translated in Alfred H. Barr Jr., *Picasso: Fifty Years of His Art*, 1946.

believe so strongly in the arts as a bridge to a new way of thinking, to a new life.

As children, we're fascinated by shapes, sounds, and colors. Later, we focus our attention on things that frighten us, delight us, intrigue us, or make us feel secure. "When my daughter was about seven years old," says artist and art professor Howard Ikemoto, "she asked me one day what I did at work. I told her I worked at the college—my job was to teach people how to draw. She stared back at me, incredulous, and said, 'You mean they forget?'"

We do forget. In fact, we are taught to forget, and to replace the simple, natural pragmatism of a child with a more "serious," grown-up approach to life. We're told how complicated life is, told we can't do this and we're not smart enough or fast enough or talented enough to pursue that. And in hearing that—in responding to these words whose effect is to close doors and narrow our thinking—we make ourselves poor, sometimes just as poor in our imagination and in leading a meaningful life as the folks I work with in Manchester. We're told how difficult things are and how far they are beyond our reach. And that's wrong.

It's important to be responsible with your life, to have vision, ambition, and some idea of what you want to be. But I believe that we can place so much trust in what the world tells us is sensible that we lose the chance to live extraordinary lives. True artists never make that mistake. The way they set priorities can teach us all a lesson about how to live a meaningful life. Imagine, for example, a young man who sets out to become an artist, following the conventional, "practical" path. He has obvious talent—with an eye for shape and proportion, a good sense of color and composition, he can paint, he can draw. His gifts are so clear that a career in art seems obvious. He gets into a good art school, masters the techniques, studies various styles and trends. Finally, it comes time to paint his masterpieces and establish his reputation. What should he paint? Landscapes? Portraits? A still life? A still life, then. Next, what should his subject be? Flowers? What kind? He does some research and finds out that a lot of people love sunflowers. Okay, sunflowers it is. He learns all he can about sunflowers. He reads textbooks. He questions experts. He dissects a few sunflowers to see how they're put together. Finally, he sits down to paint.

What he produces might well be technically flawless, but what are the chances it will be *art*? He hasn't built his life around art, or around capturing the essence of a flower. Instead, he channeled his talent to achieve a predetermined goal. When he looks for the beauty and meaning within the flower, all he is likely to find is the blind ambition that brought him this far.

Now imagine a young Vincent van Gogh wandering the countryside, drinking in the beauty he sees all around him. He picks up a pencil and teaches himself to draw. Later, he tries his hand at painting. He fails at first, suffers doubts and setbacks, but he never quits, because he has no choice. He strives to develop the skills he needs to express the beauty he feels in his soul. One day, after teaching himself to paint, he sees a sunflower. He doesn't try to justify the way the flower makes him feel. He doesn't need someone's validation to know that the feeling is important. He simply trusts the feeling. He explores it, tries to capture the feeling on canvas. And in the process he creates a masterpiece. The painting he produces is about more than mere sunflowers. The sunflower was a gateway for Van Gogh; it opened his eyes to the explosion of color and life and energy within. When I first laid eyes on an orchid, I too recognized it as a gateway. I was no Van Gogh, but I didn't have to be. Neither do you. We only have to pay attention and strive to recognize the passion when it occurs.

"The greatest work of an artist is the history of a painting," said the Renaissance artist Leon Battista Alberti. What he means, I think, is that a work of art is something more than a product of talent, technique, and vision. It's an expression of all the life experiences that enable the artist to be a person capable of creating a particular piece of art. In other words, the job of an artist is to live a life. In purely human terms, the art on canvas is secondary, almost inconsequential, compared to the art of living.

We're taught that the practical path to a successful life is to create clear goals, then develop the tactics and strategies to reach them. We're told we need to have some sense of direction in our lives, and that we need to have the discipline and vision to make our dreams come true. But too often, a goal becomes a tyrant. It turns you into a runner in a race, following a course someone else has laid out. Your vision narrows. You race by any number of interesting side streets, full of the unexpected, but you don't even see them because your eye is fixed too firmly on the finish line.

That is where impossibility thinking comes in. My own life is a perfect example of someone following these side streets. I worked hard at Pitt to earn an education degree, which I hoped would lead to a career as a history teacher. I never used that degree. I never taught history a day in my life. If I had been a slave to that goal, I would have to call myself a failure. Had I single-mindedly pursued that goal, I might have brushed off the chance to run that little arts center on Buena Vista Street. But something about that opportunity captured my attention in the same way that first orchid did. And I realized that being a teacher was not my deepest desire. It was just the tip of the iceberg for me. I wanted to bring meaning into my life by making the lives of others better. All the things that mattered to me, the things that I could have brushed off as impractical distractions, were signposts pointing to that deeper passion. Trusting those signposts led me to the life I have today. I trusted in the beauty of orchids and a greenhouse materialized. I trusted jazz and I wound up with a music hall for some of the top jazz musicians in the country and a music label that has won four Grammys. I trusted clay and it turned my life around and made possible the creation of the Manchester Bidwell Center, where I see lives changed every day of the week.

There's a student I'll never forget—an African-American woman, the mother of a couple of kids, who came to us straight from the county jail. She was hooked on crack cocaine before she came here, and for years her addiction drained her hope, hollowed her soul, and led her down into virtually every danger and indignity the streets had to offer. Often, her activities landed her in jail. The last time she was arrested was on a Christmas Eve. She sobered up in a jail cell, and as her mind cleared she thought of her kids at home, without her, missing their Christmas because she cared more for her habit than she did for them. Her heart broke. She hit bottom. When a judge gave her the choice of doing prison time or signing up for a job-training program at Bidwell, she chose to come see us. It wasn't an instant success. She showed up with the hardness and skepticism we see all the time. Her life on the streets had taught her some harsh lessons—about what she was capable of and what was expected of her and what she could hope for. Everything in her environment drove home the message that lies at the heart of what it means to be poor: *You don't matter; you have nothing to offer.* That's the takeaway of life in the ghetto, and it seemed so real to her that she'd call you a fool if you tried to talk her out of it. We didn't try to talk her out of anything. We put her in the culinary program. We gave her a crisp white uniform to wear and a professionally equipped kitchen to work in. She saw other people—women just like her—taking the work seriously, graduating from the program, landing decent jobs. I don't know when, exactly, she bought into the program, but she kept herself off drugs and she showed up every day. I knew what was happening because I'd seen it a thousand times before: She was shifting her frame of reference. "Possibility" wasn't out in the street anymore, it was in the mixing bowl in front of her, in the lump of dough she was working with her hands. She had a new way of looking at her future now, something she could shape with her effort and her talent. She wasn't limited by the practical wisdom that had shaped her life for so long. She was trusting something else—the feeling of hope and possibility she felt each time she turned out a beautiful loaf of bread or a single perfect pastry. That became the proof she needed to work toward a better future.

That woman completed her training with flying colors, and when the term ended her classmates chose her to speak as their representative at the graduation ceremony. The music hall was full when she took the stage. She used the opportunity to speak directly to her children, who were sitting in the audience. We were all moved to silence as she poured out her heart to her kids. "I am sorry I was always out feeding my habit," she said, "when I should have been home feeding you." The kids ran up to the stage and embraced their mother. She promised them a better future, a better life together. And she delivered. She landed a job as assistant chef in a prominent local restaurant. She kept herself clean and sober and is now a model of strength and responsibility for her kids. Now they have a much better chance of living good lives themselves. The struggles that woman faced were extreme, but we can all learn something from them. She changed her life by learning to see past the folks who told her what she could not be, placing her trust in the power and possibility she already held in her hands.

"It takes immense genius," says the novelist Edmond Duranty, "to represent, simply and sincerely, what we see in front of us." But that kind of genius isn't beyond our reach. All we have to do is learn to trust the wisdom that is already in our hearts.

It's my habit to stop in at the greenhouse every now and then and pick up a few orchids to take home. One afternoon I walked into the place and saw two women talking. One of them was one of our students, a young African-American woman from an inner-city neighborhood who was close to graduating from the horticulture program. The other was a very poised and polished white woman, obviously affluent and educated, who was visiting the greenhouse as part of an event involving a local orchid society. They were discussing an orchid the young black woman was holding. What struck me was their body language: The black woman was doing all the talking, pointing at the flower, lifting the petals up and down. She was teaching the white woman about the orchid. The white woman, who was the taller of the two, bent down a little in a posture of attentiveness. She nodded as the black woman spoke to show she was taking it all in. I knew the world our student had come from, and I knew a little about the world where the white woman lived. The overlap between these worlds is virtually nonexistent. If their paths had somehow crossed, they would have passed each other without notice. But inside the greenhouse, there was no rich and poor, no class or race or what neighborhood you were from. It was all about the orchid. It was a moment of growth and transformation, with a mountain of assumptions being washed away, as the poor woman from the inner city told the rich woman from the suburbs what she needed to know to care properly for the delicate flower.

Sometimes I wonder what would have happened if I had scaled back my dreams, tried to be more practical, and aimed for more conventional goals—in other words, if I had limited myself to the possible. It might have led to a comfortable life. But there would be no greenhouse, no Grammy Awards, no Manchester Bidwell. It would have been extremely unlikely that those women in the greenhouse would have ever met. But I didn't scale back, and the moment I fell in love with that orchid, that meeting in the greenhouse was already a done deal.

That limitless possibility is what all of us deserve. I wish I could say I knew in advance that we could solve some of the problems in our society by growing a tropical flower on some of the bleakest streets in the city. But it didn't happen that way. It happened because I trusted the intuition that told me I needed the beauty of orchids in my life. Now, every time I stop at the greenhouse to pick up some orchids to take home, I am struck by the same simple thought that started it all, the same thought I was thinking the first time I laid eyes on an orchid.

Damn, that's a beautiful flower.

CHAPTER SEVEN

The Power of Passion

was twenty-four years old, running the Manchester Craftsmen's Guild on Buena Vista Street, when I took my first trip on a plane. It was a flight to Boston to visit a girl I had met who worked at the Harvard Business School. On the flight, all around me people were dozing, reading magazines, or chatting with one another. Most were seasoned passengers, I guess; for them the flight was just a matter of killing time as they traveled. For me it was a miracle. This was back when commercial airline travel still possessed an aura of privilege and glamour. Everything about the experience—the confident bearing of the pilots, the practiced poise and competence of the flight attendants, the functional comfort of the cabin, even the sounds and sensations of flight—was exciting. I sat in a window seat, and for much of the flight I couldn't take my eyes off the view. It was winter down below, but above the clouds the sun was shining and we were surrounded by nothing but bright blue air; the way the wings caught the sunshine made my heart soar. *I'm flying, man,* I told myself. *I'm inside a metal tube, traveling at 500 miles per hour, 30,000 feet above the ground!*

As I looked out the window, I remembered a story my mother used to tell about something I said when I was small. We were sitting in the yard of our house, and I was looking up at a sky full of dramatic cloud formations opening up to sudden patches of blue. "I'm going up there someday," I said. My brash assurance made my mother laugh, and she reminded me of it many times as I grew. But I noticed there was always a wistfulness in her voice when she told that story, for she knew that Manchester was not the most likely platform from which a child could reach for the sky.

When the plane neared the Boston airport and we began our descent, the horizon rolled out below me like an endless scale model of the world, with perfect little towns, farms, rivers, bridges. I loved the feel of the big plane as it skipped on the wind a little and banked into its final descent. I heard the thump and whir of the landing gear dropping as the pilots leveled the plane for the airport approach, the thrill of the land rising up to meet us, the aircraft hanging one last second, wings swaying, then leveling, and the tires touching down as the plane landed smoothly on the runway and the engines roared in reverse to slow us down.

It all took my breath away. For a moment, I sat back in my seat, struck by a familiar sense of wonder and recognition. It was similar to the feeling I got the day I first walked into Mr. Ross's classroom, the feeling I had the first time jazz got under my skin and sent my spirits flying. It's the feeling, I now understand, that tips you off to the fact that you are staring into the face of a newly discovered passion. We all face those moments all the time. The trick is to spot them and give them some attention before they drift away, out of sight and out of mind. So when the plane had taxied to the gate, I didn't grab for my carry-on bag and scramble for the door. Instead, I sat with the feeling for a while. Flying was one of the hippest, most exciting experiences I'd ever had. I had made up my mind. I wanted more of it in my life. But I didn't mean I wanted to be a passenger more often. I wanted to be a pilot. I was going to learn to fly.

Moments later, I was at the front of the plane, where I met the pilot standing in the aisle. I stuck out my hand. "Hi," I said, "I'm Bill Strickland. How do I get a job like yours?" I wasted no time thinking about the audacity of what I was asking: A few hours earlier, I had never seen the inside of a commercial aircraft, and now I wanted to fly one. The pilot and copilot chuckled good-naturedly, thinking I was making a joke. So I stood there intently until they could see I was serious. They could have dismissed me as a fool, but for some reason, they didn't. "It's not an easy job to get," the pilot said. "Competition is stiff. But if you're serious, the first step is to get your private pilot's license. Find a private flight school," he said. "Take some lessons. See if it's for you."

My relationship with the girl ended later, but my passion for flying remained. As soon as I got home, I opened the Yellow Pages and found a flight school based at the Allegheny County Airport, a short drive from where I lived. I enrolled, and my first few lessons convinced me that my passion for flying was real. So I kept showing up at the airport. I took lessons in small single-engine planes until I learned to solo, and eventually I earned my private pilot's license. Now I could fly anytime I wanted. But I was after more than that—I wanted to fly commercial jets for a living, and that required me to qualify for a commercial pilot's license, a difficult certification to earn. When word of my dreams got around, I became an endless source of humor for the other pilots at the flight school.

"Do you have any idea what you're up against?" they'd say. "Top-gun types, fighter pilots, guys who have been flying military transports for years. What chance do you have, flying these little planes?" I ignored them. I wasn't going to let them dampen my spirits. Anyway, there was a more serious threat to my dreams in the form of some simple but sobering math: To qualify for a commercial license, I'd have to log at least 1,000 hours of flying time. Planes rented for fifty bucks an hour. On my modest salary, there was no way I could come up with the $50,000 needed to pay for that much flight time.

There are times when life gives you a wake-up call and forces you to examine your dreams with unvarnished clarity. For many, it's a time when a lot of dreams die. It would have been admirably sensible of me, in that moment, to scale back my hopes. After all, I was a pilot already; I could rent a plane and fly around for fun anytime I wanted. But that wasn't my dream. My dream was to fly big commercial jets full of passengers to the four corners of the earth, and my dream wouldn't let me rest. That's what true passion does. It lifts your vision above the safe and the sensible and gives you the guts or the foolhardiness to do something outrageous when only the outrageous will do. It draws your eye to opportunities you would otherwise miss.

That's what happened to me at the airport. One night after a lesson, as I was leaving the school, I drove past the open door of a hangar. Inside was an airplane, a sleek, single-engine Beech Sundowner, and on the door of the hangar was a sign that read "Airplane for Sale." I'd passed that plane a half dozen times before and hardly noticed it. But I noticed it now, and as I looked it over an outrageous possibility occurred to me. When I got home, I called about the Sundowner. The asking price was $50,000. It struck me that my flight school might need another plane for training, so I called and asked the owner if he'd be interested in leasing a plane from me. He said he'd be willing if the terms were right. The next day, I took his willingness to the bank—literally. I told the loan officer I wanted to buy an airplane, then lease it back to the flight school for a monthly fee that would cover my loan payments. The math added up, so they loaned me the money. I bought the Sundowner and leased it to the school. Then I used the plane, when it wasn't being rented out, to accumulate the flight time I needed. The flight school maintained the plane, and the money from the lease paid back my loan. My only expense was the cost of fuel. I was flying almost for free. I couldn't have dreamed up that plan if I'd been thinking "sensibly." Good sense would have told me that my dream was impossible, and when the mind accepts impossibility, the game is over. But that's the power of genuine passion—it ignores the impossible and gives you the drive you need to do whatever you have to do to make a dream come true, no matter how extreme, or unlikely, or absurd those actions might seem. It *was* absurd for me to own an airplane—I didn't even own a house at the time. But experience has taught me, again and again, that sometimes the most impractical, irresponsible, unconventional move turns out to be the one that makes the most sense.

That's not to say that doors fly open to you as soon as you muster the courage to follow a passion. Often, being true to a passion forces you to endure more than your share of defeat and discouragement. But, at the same time, when your dreams are rooted in the things you care for most, you naturally find the strength and determination you need to prevail. The flight time I logged in the Sundowner helped me earn my commercial pilot's license, but when I hit the streets with that license in hand, looking for a job, I was turned down by every airline I approached. It was a devastating setback. To say I was disappointed doesn't begin to describe my feelings. Were all the naysayers right? Was my dream of flying commercial jets too unrealistic, too outrageous? I couldn't make myself accept that. So instead of giving up on the dream or scaling back my aspirations, I made the dream bigger. I decided to earn my flight engineer's certification, which I knew would give me a much better chance at landing a pilot's job. There was a good flight school in Atlanta, but tuition was high; the school would eat up all my modest savings and plunge me into debt. Taking that risk could have been the most irresponsible thing I could do, but I trusted the dream and was determined to make it happen.

Does that mean I wasn't troubled by self-doubt? Of course not. In Atlanta, I found myself competing with hotshot fighter pilots fresh out of the military, piloting jets that were twenty times bigger and five times faster than anything I'd ever flown. It was an intimidating, pressure-packed environment, and every time I made a mistake—a mistake that in a real flight situation might cost hundreds of passengers their lives—I had to ask myself if I really belonged there. One morning I was flying copilot in a flight simulator, which provides an intensely realistic experience of what it feels like to handle a big plane, when a bell on the instrument panel started chiming urgently. I felt my seat shift and sink beneath me, as if our forward momentum had been lost. I had made a serious mistake. I had bungled what pilots call "the angle of attack." In simple terms, the only thing that keeps a plane in the sky is the aerodynamic lift produced by the smooth flow of air over the wings. I'd let the plane wobble into an awkward angle in which that flow was interrupted.

"You stalled it," said my flight instructor. In a real plane, we'd now be in danger of falling from the sky. You can't always right a stalled aircraft, and some anxious moments followed. But with my instructor's help, I fought us back into the proper angle and ended the simulated flight safely with a successful landing. I left that exercise with some serious misgivings, though. I should have anticipated the possibility that the plane could stall and focused my attention on maintaining the proper angle of attack. But I dropped my guard and never saw it coming. In real life that mistake might have killed me, along with maybe 200 passengers. That slipup rocked my confidence to the core. Was I fooling myself? Was I wasting my time and all the money I had on an irresponsible fantasy? Maybe I should face reality, cut my losses, and head back home. I had given my best shot to make my dream come true, but maybe it was time to accept the fact that my best might not be good enough.

Those questions kept me up half the night. But when I woke up in the morning and looked in the mirror, I still saw a guy who believed he could be a pilot. My passion simply wouldn't let me see myself as a failure. It wouldn't allow me to use my mistakes and shortcomings as excuses to quit. One of the distinguishing factors of a true passion, I believe, is that it never allows you to accept the excuse of failure. Failure is a function of ambition. You fail when you fall short of some specific goal. You didn't measure up and as a result success has passed you by. In such a scenario, a failure is something that you *become.* But passion isn't something that you strive for. It's part of you. It's never out of reach, and no matter how many times you stumble in your effort to embrace it, it's always there, giving you the chance to take another shot.

The next time I went up with my instructor, he taught me not to wait for the warning chime before reacting to a stall. Your stomach will feel the stall before the instruments detect it, he said. He taught me to recognize that feeling and trust it, and he showed me how to react when it occurred—ease off the yoke smoothly, get the nose down, get the air flowing smoothly over the wing. Act fast and there's nothing to worry about. I never worried about stalling again.

The fear of failure can stifle anyone's dream of living an extraordinary life. And the way you overcome that fear is by trusting your passion. Passion won't protect you against setbacks, but it will ensure that no failure is ever final. Setbacks become learning experiences. They give you the chance to refine your vision, rethink your approach, and develop the skills and values you need to achieve the things you're after. Most important, they remind you how much your dreams mean to you and give you the chance to strengthen your commitment to making those dreams come true.

Six weeks after earning my flight engineer's credentials, I landed a pilot's job with Braniff Airlines, the hippest airline going. My job required me to fly only on weekends, which allowed me to spend weekdays running the Craftsmen's Guild. But every Friday afternoon I'd change out of the rugged work clothes that were my outfit as an urban artist to put on the crisply pressed uniform of a Braniff Airlines pilot, and in hours would be flying domestic routes out of New York or making occasional trips to Acapulco, Bogotá, and other exotic destinations in Central and South America. Flying commercial jets was everything I'd thought it would be: For me every flight was an adventure. I'll never forget the adrenaline rush of my first time in the cockpit as a member of a commercial flight crew. I was the flight engineer, in charge of all flight systems and power settings. My heart pounded as the packed 727 lifted its nose and headed up through the clouds toward a distant patch of blue. Soon after we touched down, I found a phone and called my mother. "Hi, Mom," I said. "Remember that blue sky I said I was going to fly in one day? Well, I finally made it."

I was driven to that achievement, in part, by purely ambitious goals—I liked thinking about the salary, the prestige, the pride I'd feel when I'd walk around Manchester in my pilot's uniform. But those ambitions were grounded in my passion—a passion for flying—and it was the passion that led me to achieve my dreams. Ambition alone could never have given me the vision and the staying power I needed to make my dream come true. Sheer ambition does have benefits, but they are limited. It focuses your vision, but it narrows it, too. It gives you a tangible goal to shoot for, but the fear of falling short of a goal can rob you of the boldness and broad vision you need to achieve a truly audacious goal. You can't fall short of passion, because passion is here and now, it's something you already own. When it remains, strong and insistent, no matter how many setbacks you suffer, you continue to pick yourself up and try again. Passion isn't blunted by defeat. It isn't tamed by common sense or conventional expectations. Passions have no practical purpose—their only purpose is your passion itself. But trusting and exploring your passions can have a tremendous effect, because they engage your mind and imagination in a way that forces you to surmount any number of practical concerns and achieve the extraordinary.

I believe each of us, every human being, has the potential to do remarkable things. I see proof of that at Manchester Bidwell every day. And I'm convinced that passion is the most powerful tool we have for tapping that potential. Passion demands faith and creativity. It deepens motivation and sharpens one's eye for opportunity. Passions force us to define our values and to develop the strengths and skills we need to realize our dreams. Ambition points the way to some vaguely possible future, but too often, those hopes are shaped by someone else's idea of what our life should be. But a life based on real passion grows organically, the way the growth of a tree is guided by its need for sunshine and rain. The true power of passion lies in its ability to shape our life into something remarkable and unique. Passions do more than give us a vision of what a life can be; they force us to find the values, strengths, and skills we need to become the kind of person we are meant to be.

One of the most empowering characteristics of passion is that it drives us to develop new skills.

My job as CEO of Manchester Bidwell demands a mastery of all the skills of leadership and business administration that executives in any business enterprise must possess. I oversee all aspects of our operation—management, development, fund-raising, and community relations. I build and maintain strong partnerships with large corporations. I am required to interact with those at the highest levels of government, the educational system, and the corporate world. But I wasn't born knowing how to do all those things—not in Manchester, not by a long shot. And I didn't learn how to do any of it in school— as you know, I don't have an M.B.A. and I never studied management. I never took a business class in my life. I figured it out along the way because I *had* to just to stay afloat. That's the practical effect of passion. That is the power of what passion for what you do can do for you. Talent without passion is rudderless. But passion, when coupled with even the most rudimentary skills and a deep desire to learn, can accomplish miracles.

When I was getting Manchester Craftsmen's Guild off the ground— as a nineteen-year-old kid with no business background whatsoever— the Reverend Tom Cox and his boss, Bishop Appleyard, thought it would be a good idea to get someone to guide me through the basics of running the operation. And this is perhaps the second secret to success—having the assistance of experienced colleagues or strong mentors. No one accomplishes great things without the help of a lot of others. It just can't be done. They hooked me up with lawyers at Reed, Smith, Shaw & McClay, one of the most prestigious law firms in town, who agreed to work with me to set up the basics of a well-organized nonprofit organization. They quickly realized that my business education would have to start at rock bottom. One of the first things they had me do was fill out some federal tax forms. I filled them out by hand, in ballpoint pen, and sent them to a Reed, Smith secretary. She sent them back with a kind note gently suggesting I do the forms again on a typewriter. That note stung like a slap in the face; I was mortified by the lack of professionalism I had shown. But I learned an important lesson: Now I was beginning to understand that such a thing as professionalism existed.

At first, all the lessons were that basic. I learned how to balance the books, how to file taxes, how to keep track of materials and supplies. Before long, I had acquired the business skills I needed to lead that modest operation and keep my dream alive. The Craftsmen's Guild had become what I wanted it to be, and I could have been happy for years running the place just as it was. But my passion wanted more. That's what genuine passion can do for you—push you to broaden your vision, to deepen your experience, to seek out bigger and more complex dreams. So several years later I took the job at Bidwell, too. I got my pilot's license. I built the Manchester Bidwell Center that exists today. Each time my dream grew I was forced to take new risks, develop new capabilities, test my values and my purpose again. Today, on any given day, I might go from breakfast with the governor of Pennsylvania to a business lunch with a group of corporate CEOs. In the afternoon, I may have a meeting of one of the corporate boards I sit on, and perhaps meet with school board officials to discuss how our programs are doing in the schools.

I am now sought after by businesses across the country that think their employees might benefit from hearing my thoughts about management and leadership. One of the key points I try to offer, one of the things those I work with know about me, is that I didn't acquire my leadership expertise to satisfy some personal ambition. It wouldn't have worked—it wouldn't have been enough. I didn't pursue a set of skills or a training program, then try to market myself to the world. I just followed the lead of the things that inspired and excited me, and I learned what I needed to know from the bottom up, from the inside out, on an as-needed basis, as the survival of the dream required. That's what passion does—it shapes your life naturally, organically, the way the growth of a tree is shaped by the need for sunlight and rain.

Passion also helps us generate the courage we need to accomplish our dreams. Trusting in a passion requires a long leap of faith, and a leap of faith can be a frightening thing. But if the passion is strong enough, it will give you an irresistible reason to find the courage to face any challenges that stand in your way. It won't settle for less. In my work I deal with lots of troubled lives, and more than once I have had to stand in the way of desperate people, and occasionally some genuinely bad actors, to keep them from hurting themselves or someone else. I never set out to be a hero; it was my belief in my work that gave me the strength to do those things and kept me coming back to work every day.

One afternoon at the old Bidwell Center, I looked up to see an angry group of our trade school students forcing their way into our offices. A couple of them had guns. They were former convicts who were receiving stipends from the state while they attended our school. The state had entrusted us with handing out these stipends, but one week, because of a computer failure in the state capital, the checks did not arrive, and the men in my office were not happy. They held Jesse and me at gunpoint and demanded their money on the spot. We told them we didn't have any money to give them, which only made them angrier, and things were deteriorating fast. Luckily for us, word about the trouble had gotten out on the street, and before long we heard a commotion in the hallway. Moments later, a small brigade of women—mothers from the neighborhood—barged in and stood between us and our captors. Those ex-cons were hard guys, but they weren't ready to stand up to the scorn and disapproval of those strong ladies. The women stared them down and saved our butts. But I had to think long and hard about showing up for work the next day. I knew some influential people by then—in government, in education, in Pittsburgh's corporate and foundation communities—and with a little luck and effort I could have found a much easier and safer way to make a living. But in the end, I never thought seriously about giving up the work I was doing. It was my life, not a career; if I walked away from it, I'd be walking away from the things that made me who I am.

So I showed up for work in the morning, more committed than ever to what we were trying to do at Bidwell. And my only change was to try even harder to make the place work.

That was not the only time I feared for my physical safety, but thankfully such experiences have been rare. More commonly, the challenges I face have forced me to summon a subtler kind of courage—the courage to endure, to grow, to make myself vulnerable to the risks and uncertainties of new opportunities and unfamiliar worlds. For example, as part of their campaign to get me off to a sound start at the Craftsmen's Guild, Tom Cox and Bishop Appleyard did all they could to connect me with people in the local power structure who might be willing to help me. One of the most powerful of all those people was Drew Mathieson, one of the original architects of Mellon Financial Corporation and a board member, and future head, of the Mellon Foundation, one of the largest charitable foundations in the world.

At the bishop's suggestion, Drew agreed to have lunch with me. He invited me to meet him in the downtown financial district at his favorite place, the Duquesne Club. The Duquesne Club is the oldest and most prestigious private club in Pittsburgh. Its membership has comprised the city's power elite since the days of the great robber barons; some swear you can still smell Andrew Carnegie's cigar smoke when you walk in. I was startled by the invitation to meet there. At the time, women visitors were still required to enter the club through a side door, and I didn't think they let black people in at all, even as kitchen staff. That morning, I changed out of my usual Craftsmen's Guild uniform—combat boots, army fatigue pants, and a T-shirt—and put on my only suit.

Less than an hour later, I walked into the club and looked around. The place was just what I expected—dark wood paneling, paintings of hunting scenes on the walls, men in dark suits sitting in leather club chairs, smoking cigars and reading the *Wall Street Journal*. I felt as if I had walked into an old *New Yorker* cartoon, with the weight of all that history and tradition—all that wealthy, white tradition—pressing down on me. *What am I doing here?* I asked myself. *What do I have to say to a guy like this?* I felt so out of place, it alarmed me. I knew there must be an unofficial code of conduct here—subtle signals of dress, speech, taste, and mannerism that identify you to others as someone who belongs. I knew nothing about that code, and that put me on treacherous ground. Humiliation was a real possibility here; all it would take would be one social gaffe and the man who could connect me to all the power I needed to make my little school succeed would write me off as just some bumpkin from the ghetto. My heart pounded and my survival instincts told me to head for the door, but I knew there was too much to be gained, so I steadied myself, signaled a waiter, and moments later I was sitting at Mr. Mathieson's table.

"What would you like to drink?" he asked me. I had no idea what the possibilities were, but I didn't want Drew to see that, so I waited until he ordered, then asked for the same. I used the same strategy when it was time to order our food. We chatted as we waited for lunch to arrive, but my attention was diverted by the astonishing array of silverware flanking the plate in front of me. I'd never seen so many forks. But I knew they weren't there as decoration. I could see from the various sizes, shapes, and number of tines that each fork had its purpose and that choosing the wrong fork at the wrong time would brand me as a clueless kid. So as that lunch progressed, I played a secret game of follow the leader, stalling for time until Drew picked up a fork, then casually following his lead.

Looking back, I'm sure Drew was on to my little game, and in a way, I think it impressed him. It showed him I was a sincere and serious person, that I had an awareness of what I was getting into and an earnest desire to understand how the game of power is played. We hit it off. He asked about my plans for the center. I told him what Frank Ross had done for me and that I wanted to pass that gift on to neighborhood kids. Drew agreed to help. Then he introduced me to other members of the club. I could see the questions in their eyes when they met me, wondering who I was and how I'd gotten there. I may have been the first young black man they'd ever seen at the club, but I didn't sense any hostility or disapproval. I sensed interest and curiosity. They must have been thinking, *I don't know where this kid came from, but he must have something going on if he's having lunch with Drew Mathieson.*

I liked being looked at that way, and I tried to learn whatever I could from those guys. I noticed the kinds of drinks they ordered, what they ate for lunch, the way they leaned forward slightly and stared into your eyes when they shook your hand, their ties, their shoes, the cut of their suits. It would have been easy to write those guys off as a bunch of white fat cats, part of the culture that had held my people down. But my mother hadn't brought me up that way. She taught me to see the potential, the goodness, in all people. What I saw in these folks was confidence and power, and I intuitively understood that it was power that could help me do something good. I wanted to understand as much as I could about those guys. I wanted them to see me as a serious person with something to offer. I wanted them to want to know my dreams and to understand why they should want to help me make my dreams come true.

Drew and I ended the lunch with an agreement to meet again. Then a waiter placed a small ceramic bowl in front of me. It was full of clear liquid, with a lemon slice floating on top. *What is this,* I wondered, *soup? I thought we were finished.* I was about to reach for a spoon, but instinct told me to wait. Then I saw Drew dip his fingertips into his bowl and dry them off. I nonchalantly did the same, pretending I'd been dealing with finger bowls in Manchester all my life. On the way back to my car, I passed a Brooks Brothers store. There was a dark blue suit in the window, the same suit almost every guy at the Duquesne Club was wearing. Then I saw my own reflection in the plate glass, saw how I looked in the inexpensive suit I had on. On an ordinary day, walking into a Brooks Brothers store would be an intimidating experience for a black kid from the ghetto, but hell, I'd just had lunch at the Duquesne Club. I walked in and ordered one of those suits. The next time I showed up at the Duquesne Club, I wore the suit to give Drew, and all those other guys, a clear indication that I was ready to play the game at their level, on their own turf. And I think they respected me for it. The connections I formed at the Duquesne Club led to some of the strongest friendships and most productive alliances I ever had. Drew Mathieson became a mentor, a confidant, and a lifelong friend. I named the greenhouse in his honor, and when he died his wife asked me to give a eulogy at his funeral. A few days after the service I was approached by Marty McGuinn, chairman of Mellon Bank, who offered me a spot on Mellon's board of directors. He thought it was what Drew would have wanted. I accepted, and served on Mellon's board until its recent merger with Bank of New York. It was not an honorary position. I was part of Mellon's Risk Committee, which made recommendations about investments and acquisitions that could have earned or cost the bank millions of dollars. It was a position of great responsibility—and, for me, great honor. I took my first step toward that honor when I mustered the guts to walk into the Duquesne Club, into an intimidating world of class and power, as a kid who didn't own a decent suit or even know which fork to use to eat his salad. It was my passion to make my dream come true that got me to enter that world and gave me the courage to find my place in it.

But courage gets you nowhere without conviction. Here again, passion serves you well by summoning the deep resolve and self-confidence you need to make extraordinary dreams come true.

One of the reasons I'm so taken with the architecture of Frank Lloyd Wright is that so much of it is a bold, clear declaration of his artistic integrity and his refusal to abandon a dream he believes in. Wright's design for Fallingwater not only defied all conventional thinking about what a house should be, it also confounded his client's engineers, who believed the cantilevered terraces that jutted from the house were dangerously undersupported. With the consent of the clients, the engineers had the contractor extend the supporting walls by several feet without Wright's knowledge. But Wright immediately spotted the change the next time he visited the site. It altered the house in ways that Wright found unacceptable, so he convinced the contractor to secretly cut away the top four inches of the new wall. A month later, his client, Edgar Kaufmann, confessed to Wright that he had authorized the building of the new wall. Wright led him to the wall, showed him the space between the top of the wall and the terrace, and pointed out that, clearly, the wall was supporting nothing and yet the terrace showed no signs of failure. Seeing what Wright had done, Kaufmann had the new wall removed, leaving the terrace as Wright had originally intended.

Restoring that wall to its original dimensions, while experienced engineers insisted that doing so would cause a catastrophic collapse, required an incredible sense of conviction. It is the sort of conviction that can only come from true passion. Mere belief, or common sense, or ambition won't hold up in situations like this. Uncommon faith is required. If Wright had been motivated only by self-interested ambition—to complete the house, for example, and collect his fee—he would have let the altered wall stand. But Wright was determined to build the house he felt in his heart and saw in his mind. He had done his homework thoroughly and knew the house would stand. Even so, it required absolute faith in his vision and expertise to give the order to cut into that wall. Passion is the richest and most trustworthy source of that kind of conviction, and I've drawn on it time and time again as I've faced the challenges of my own life.

At every key moment in my life, someone has tried to convince me that my dreams weren't worth the risks involved, or that my vision was too grand and unconventional to ever come to fruition. *You can't grow orchids in the ghetto. You can't teach poor folks science and higher math. No white people are going to come to Manchester to hear music. A guy with no flight experience can't become an airline pilot! Poor people don't need a fountain.*

It was usually very sound and practical advice. And if I had been guided by merely the desire to live a "successful" life, I would have been wise to take it. But I wasn't after doing what was acceptable or right. I wanted to make a difference and change the world, starting with my neighborhood. Just as important, I was trying as best I could to live a life that felt genuinely like my own, and to do that I had to own up to the passions that defined me. So I ignored the naysayers and found a way to reach higher. It was never easy, but the more I trusted my passions, the more I found reason to believe that following my dreams was the most practical thing I could do. Passion also forced me to develop the determination and perseverance I needed to keep those dreams alive when times got rough and the things I wanted seemed very far away. If my life has taught me anything, it's that no genuine success is possible without an intense, tireless, and focused sense of drive. You need an incredible amount of discipline to stay focused on a challenging goal, and it is hard to maintain your level of enthusiasm through sheer will alone. No matter how important the goal may seem, your heart just isn't buying it. On the other hand, passion, by definition, *is* excitement; and focusing on passion is exactly where all of your mind and spirit want to be. In other words, it is a bottomless, self-replenishing source of motivation.

When I was a high school kid in Frank Ross's art class, and every pot I initially tried to shape flopped over, it wasn't discipline or strength of will that kept me trying. It was my passion to make something beautiful, to tap the potential I sensed inside me. Failure was not an option. It was my passion that prevented me from giving up on that dream and every dream I've had since then. I *had* to make a success of that little art center on Buena Vista Street. I *had* to become a pilot. I *had* to build Manchester Bidwell. In every one of those cases, I faced setbacks, heartbreaks, and years of unfulfilled struggle. But I couldn't give up. Struggle is part of the equation when you bet your hopes on a passion, but the passion also makes the effort worthwhile. We struggled for years to move the creation of the greenhouse closer to reality, for example, but even after we'd won the support of Senator Santorum, obstacles got in our way. After the senator's staff had drafted the legislation that would grant us the money to start construction, we only had to wait for the bill to pass. But after months of waiting, the bill had not come up for a vote. Except for some apologies about the unwieldiness of the legislative process, the senator's staff couldn't tell us why. So we looked into the matter on our own. We soon learned that congressional votes are scheduled by a single individual in a bureaucratic office on Capitol Hill. Jesse and I flew to D.C., determined to find that office. After some legwork and a lot of phone calls, we found it in a dusty corner of the basement of the Congressional Office Building. It was staffed by a lone bureaucrat, who seemed startled—and a little flattered, I think—by the fact that we had tracked him down. We sat down in his office, and he listened as I told him the Manchester Bidwell story. After that conversation, I'll never underestimate the power of a bureaucrat to think with his heart. What we said made sense to him. Before we left, he pledged to us that he'd get our bill on the docket. He did, the legislation passed, and we were able to build our greenhouse at last.

Being true to your passion may force you to stray from the conventional path and blaze new trails of your own. By its nature, passion forces you to lead, and leaders inevitably endure criticism and resistance. But it can also give you the stability and sense of direction to keep your dreams on track and lead more effectively, in the face of sometimes withering resistance and criticism. In my work at Manchester Bidwell, I've met with outright disapproval from segments of the community that have strong ideas about how inner-city poverty programs should operate and how the people who run them should behave. A lot of these folks don't like my Brooks Brothers suits. It bothers them that so many of my friends and mentors are rich and powerful white guys. They aren't comfortable with my cozy relationship with the corporate powers that be. They feel that I've somehow sold out to the very power structure that has been keeping folks in the ghetto down, but what they're really saying is that I don't live up to their idea of what *they* think I should be. I won't pretend the criticism doesn't sting. But as a leader, I have to stay focused and move past it. I'm not interested in fitting into someone else's preconceived mold. My determination to live my life with purpose, in a way that improves the lives of people who need some help to unlock their own potential, never wanes. It seems to me the old ways of social intervention aren't working. I think I found a way that helps people. If it means wearing a suit and a tie instead of my old urban uniform of army fatigues and combat boots, that's what I'm going to do. And if I have to learn the style and language of corporate America to make that world understand that helping the poor is not about charity but about improving society in ways that will yield significant benefits for their own bottom lines, then I'm going to do that, too. It's not about being popular, it's about having the guts and the integrity to be true to your vision, about caring more about the thing you're trying to achieve than your allegiances to ideology, conventional expectations, or what other people might think.

Recently, I flew out to the Midwest to meet a young African-American man who wants to start a center like Manchester Bidwell in his city. He's a smart kid, and I like his enthusiasm and sincerity, but he has a lot to learn if he wants to do some good. I didn't waste any time getting to the point with him. He met me wearing funky jeans and a T-shirt, his hair braided into pigtails. It was an artsy, urban look, and I know he meant it to show his solidarity with his roots and his commitment to the people he was trying to help. But if he wanted to model his center on mine, I had to let him know right away he needed to rethink his intentions.

"You got a suit, man?" I said as soon as I met him. "Because I can't take you to some boardroom looking like that." My bluntness rattled him, but it was something I needed to say. To move his plans forward, he'd have to convince the leaders of at least one large corporation that he was someone whose vision and competence they could trust. No corporate leaders that I know of would contribute to his cause the way he presented himself to me. You have to match up with *their* idea of someone who takes himself seriously. I didn't want him to go to those corporations as someone asking for a handout—I wanted him to go in there as someone who can deliver something the corporations need.

Was I asking him to sell out? I've left that for him to decide. If he feels he'd be selling out by changing his image, then he should continue to live his life in a way that seems most genuine to him. If he truly wants to lead, then changing his attitude, his look, and his style are part of the price he'll have to pay to make his vision real. My reaction surprised him, but a few days after we met he sent me an e-mail saying that he felt our meeting was "a rite of passage" for him. Does he have the commitment to lead, or is he just trying to make a statement with his life? We'll find out in his actions. If his passion to lead is genuine, then whatever sacrifices it requires from him will be worthwhile.

MY OWN PASSIONS have always been very clear to me, so I'm always surprised when someone admits to me that they have no defining passion in their lives. Passions aren't hard to find.

If you're paying attention to your life at all, the things you are passionate about won't leave you alone. They're the ideas and hopes and possibilities your mind naturally gravitates to, the things you would focus your time and attention on for no other reason than that doing them feels right. Passions are irresistible and restless; they tug at your sleeve, demanding your attention. It's no trick to recognize your passions. The hard part is trusting in them as an organizing principle in your life. Why is that so difficult? The problem is fear. We're afraid that following our passions will make us look impractical, ineffectual, self-indulgent, or even irresponsible. What if, for example, your passions draw you to an occupation that, to the people around you, seems foolish, or lacking in a future, or doesn't offer what they see as the necessary earning power and social prestige they expect? For me, it's another case of an illusion being mistaken for what is practical. The experiences of my life, and of so many students at our school, have convinced me beyond doubt of the practical power of passion to unlock our deepest potential. Denying your passions cuts you off from this power; it is the most impractical thing you could do. Second, never think that trusting in your passion gives you any kind of free pass through life. It doesn't excuse you from unpleasant tasks. In fact, it requires you to work harder, and it inspires you to reach higher than you would in the pursuit of a more "sensible" ambition.

Not long ago, I got a call from a friend of mine who is the chair of the board of a large Pittsburgh-based corporation. He told me his son had graduated with honors from Princeton and had been offered a coveted job at a blue-chip Wall Street investment firm. He was looking at a career that, over a lifetime, could pay him millions of dollars or even tens of millions. But as the offer was pending, the kid confessed to his father that he didn't really want a career in finance. What he really wanted, he said, was to be a chef. To his credit, the father supported his son. He knew the quality of our culinary program and was calling me to see if we'd accept his son as an apprentice, to give him a sense of what a career in the culinary arts might be like. I said we would, and that young man spent his time with us learning how to cook beside laid-off steelworkers, people working to get off welfare, and formerly homeless folks. He had conventional success handed to him like a gift-wrapped package, but he turned it down to bet his life on something that mattered to him more.

That doesn't mean that spending your life as a chef, or an artist, or an inner-city activist, for that matter, is morally superior to making a fortune on Wall Street. That's not the point at all. It's better to be an investment banker who lives her life with honesty and integrity, and in some way manages to make things a little better for the world around her, than to be, say, a teacher in some failing urban school who has no respect for the students she teaches and no faith in their potential to be anything more than they are. I'm often approached by idealistic young people on fire to do good for others, all hungry to save the world. I tell them the first step is *save yourself*. Make sure your own life is lined up right, that you know what's important to you and why it matters, before you set out to make your mark on the world. Do that, I assure them, and everything else will take care of itself. And I am convinced that is true. I never saw a meaningful life that wasn't based on passion. And I never saw a life full of passion that wasn't, in some important way, extraordinary.

CHAPTER EIGHT

Swing

When I was a senior in high school, Frank Ross took me to an annual jazz festival sponsored by the Catholic Youth Organization at a huge civic auditorium in Pittsburgh. The master of ceremonies was the great jazz pianist Billy Taylor. I didn't know him from Adam at the time, but from the moment I laid eyes on him he caught my attention. Not only was he a premier musician, he was also a noted jazz scholar and teacher, with a Ph.D. in music education, and his erudition came across in every word he spoke. But what really impressed me was the way he presented himself onstage. He was a distinguished, elegant, articulate, and highly accomplished black man, talking about jazz to a crowd of 10,000 people—most of them white—with a dignity and authority that had them hanging on his every word. Those qualities came across in his music, too.

As Dr. Taylor and his combo played, I found myself swept up so completely in the meaning and emotion of the music that the rest of the world simply faded away. Whatever worries were on my mind disappeared. I forgot the circumstances of my life entirely—what I had done before the concert and where I was going after. Nothing mattered but the moment and the music. I felt an almost euphoric rush of emotion, as if a door had opened to my future. It was as if someone had whispered in my ear that everything was going to be okay, and in that moment I somehow understood that life is simple and if you line your life up right—with your values, dreams, skills, and passions all pointing in the same direction—anything you hope for, whatever you wish, can come true. I didn't try to analyze or understand those feelings at the time, but I couldn't help but trust them. I left that concert in a state of joyful agitation, more confident that I could make something of my life. And I felt oddly certain that I hadn't seen the last of Dr. Taylor. For in some unimaginable way, I believed that I had struck a bond with him, as well. Although I was just one of thousands in the audience, somehow I sensed that he had an important role to play in my life.

Looking back, it's easy to dismiss such thoughts as New Age mumbo jumbo or as the product of wishful thinking. But at the time they were too strong, too convincing to be written off so easily. In any case, the fact is I didn't let them go. I clung to them. I cherished them. I fueled them by listening to Dr. Taylor's records and following his career.

One night, years later, at the time I was running the original Manchester Craftsmen's Guild, I stopped for a drink at a downtown jazz bar owned by my friend and Pittsburgh jazz musician Walt Harper. Walt spotted me when I walked in and waved me to the bar. "There's someone I want you to meet," he said. Standing at his side was a familiar, distinguished-looking man in glasses, dressed in a well-cut suit: It was Billy Taylor. Walt told Billy about my work at the Craftsmen's Guild, and Dr. Taylor seemed eager to hear all about it. The two of us took seats at a table and talked for almost an hour. I answered his questions about Manchester Craftsmen's Guild, then told him about seeing him in concert all those years earlier, how his music gave me hope that I could make my life what I wanted it to be. Over a beer, I poured out my feelings about art and how I was using the arts as a bridge to transform the lives of the kids who came to my school. Dr. Taylor listened attentively, and at some point in that conversation, I realized we were forging a real connection. Almost a decade had passed since I first saw him in concert, but Billy Taylor and I were becoming friends. When he left, he shook my hand. "I'm going to keep my eye on you," he said. "I think you're a young man who's going places. I'm sure we'll meet again."

During the mid-1980s, my work in Manchester got me noticed by the Bush administration and I was appointed by Nancy Hanks, then head of the National Endowment for the Arts, to chair a subcommittee of the National Council on the Arts that focused on community arts organizations. As part of that job, I was asked to present a report on neighborhood arts groups to the council's main panel. So I traveled to D.C. to present my report before the council. An impressive lineup of celebrities stared back at me from the dais, including Clint Eastwood, James Earl Jones, Judith Jamison of the Alvin Ailey American Dance Theater, and, at the end of the table, Dr. Taylor. After the presentation, Dr. Taylor and I renewed our acquaintanceship. He congratulated me on my talk and told me he was pleased to see what I'd accomplished. A year later, Dr. Taylor resigned his seat on the council, and thanks in part to his recommendation, I was appointed to sit on the council's main panel. It was a position that has opened up a world of new possibilities and connections for me and for Manchester Bidwell.

Dr. Taylor would play an even more meaningful role in my life. But before recounting that, I want to revisit the moment when my relationship with Billy Taylor began in that sold-out auditorium, in that remarkable moment of insight and connection, before we ever met. What was the meaning of that moment? And what can one make of the fact that my unlikely premonitions about Billy Taylor came true? Was it just a series of lucky coincidences? Perhaps. But I believe that by falling into a state of mind where I knew so clearly what I wanted, and believed so completely that what I wanted would come true, I somehow influenced my future and steered myself in the direction of Dr. Taylor.

Of course, meeting Billy Taylor was a lucky break, but someone wise once said that luck favors the prepared mind. When I met Dr. Taylor at Walt Harper's place that night, I knew, on some level, that I'd been preparing myself for that meeting for years. I had prepared myself to be the kind of person who could sit down and have something to say to a man like Billy Taylor, and that forced me to grapple with who I was, and to figure out what I really wanted my life to add up to. When Billy heard me speak, he saw me as someone who was serious about life, who had weighed his priorities and had sincerely tested his values. He recognized me as a person who was determined to live a life that mattered. Seeing that, I think, he decided I was the kind of guy who was naturally a part of his world. That night at the CYO concert, it was as if all the mental and emotional clutter of my life—all the self-doubts and insecurities, all the assumptions I'd been making about who I was and what my life could be—were momentarily swept away. In that remarkable moment I understood very clearly that the things I wanted most in life—meaning, purpose, dignity, and accomplishment—were not only possible, they were inevitable, as long as I could find the courage to be who I needed to be and act on those dreams. These insights didn't come to me as thoughts or ideas—I *felt* them. For those few brief moments, I *lived* them. I was seeing an emotional portrait of what my life could feel like. It gave me a personal, visceral reason to believe. I wasn't quite the same person afterward.

Since that first time the night at the concert, I've fallen into that same state of mind many times—while I'm working on pots, or tending my garden, or listening to jazz, or meeting someone whose life touches mine—and each time I emerge with a sharper understanding of who I am and what matters to me, and a clearer idea of how to make the life I want to live come true. The great psychologist Abraham Maslow called such moments "peak experiences" and saw them as a gateway to deep personal insight. Mythologist Joseph Campbell spoke of moments of "rapture" and famously urged his students to "follow your bliss." Noted researcher Mihaly Csikszentmihalyi wrote a classic book about the experience in which he gave it its most familiar name: "flow." I've always used a more casual term to describe the experience and the larger effect it has had on my life. I call it "swing." Swing is a term used by jazz musicians to describe those transcendent moments of musical alignment when rhythm, harmony, and melody all fall into a sweet convergence, when each member of the band anticipates what every other member is doing and gives him the help he needs to get it done; when every note you need to play matches up precisely with your ability to play it; when the music no longer requires any thought or effort, but simply streams out of your fingers and heart and through the valves of the horn or the strings of the bass or the keys of the keyboard as a natural expression of who you are. That sense of flow, those moments of freedom, conviction, gratification, and joy, are what jazz musicians live for. I've taught myself to live for them, too. We all can. And we should.

To my mind, a life that swings is the only kind of life worth living. I've spent some time talking about the elements I feel are essential to living a successful life: the clarity of vision to see what a remarkable thing it is to be alive, and to appreciate the raw potential every life offers. The need to trust the small, transcendent experiences of your life, because they show you how to build a life based on not just achievement, other people's expectations, wealth, or position, but on meaning. The need to explore your passions and draw from them the inspirational fire and fuel that make extraordinary achievements possible. Each of those elements, on its own, is a powerful tool for shaping a life. But when they converge, when clarity, trust, and passion, and the vision, strengths, and values they give you, fall into a harmonic alignment with an inner sense of what you want your life to be, they add up to that remarkable state of mind I call swing. Swing is the real engine that drives an exceptional life.

Creating moments that swing is not a difficult thing. I've learned to cultivate them in simple, reliable ways; I depend upon them to remind me of who I am and to give me the strength I need to keep doing what I'm doing. Swing can carry you past defeat and discouragement. It can reinvigorate your spirit, renew your commitment to your goals, and lift you out of whatever funk or depression or frustration that is keeping you from moving a dream forward. If you set your mind to it, you can learn to conjure up swinging moments on demand. I try to find them on a daily basis, because I have learned that one brief moment that swings can salvage an otherwise miserable day. In many ways, these refreshing, reinforcing, and clarifying moments are their own reward. But I've also learned to rely on them as a bottomless source of energy, motivation, creativity, and even luck. I treasure these moments because I like the way they make me feel.

It's the act of seeking them out that has made all the difference in my life. There's no doubt in my mind that almost every good thing I've accomplished has come as the direct or indirect result of my efforts to make my life swing.

WHEN THE MANCHESTER BIDWELL CENTER that exists today opened in 1986, anyone who knew me could see straight off that the place was built to offer our students the same rich experiences that had turned my life around. There was clay. There were art and photography. After a while, there were gourmet food and flowers.

Even the technical courses contributed to the synergy and creative cross-pollination. And it was all housed in a sleek, clean, sunlit space that had been meticulously designed down to the last detail, to give our students the same sense of self-worth and possibility that Frank Ross's classroom had nurtured in me.

From the day we opened the doors, I knew the center was going to work. We were going to transform lives. For me, however, the place was incomplete. Something was missing. I had not found a way for our beautiful new facility to incorporate jazz into the lives of our kids and adults. Jazz had always been more than mere entertainment to me. It had eased my heartbreaks, brightened my victories, validated

my aspirations, and, in a very real fashion, given me an emotional portrait of how a good, rich life should feel. And it is learning how to
capture and re-create the feelings we want in our lives that ultimately
changes our behavior and thinking. Jazz was such an integral part of
my life that I knew I had to find a way to make it a part of Manchester
Bidwell—and not just as background music piped in through the PA
system. It had to be woven into the cultural fabric of the place so it
could do for our students what it had done for me. I didn't know *how*,
specifically, it would make Manchester Bidwell stronger; I just trusted
a gut instinct that told me jazz belonged. And I had no uncertainties
about how to bring it into the mix.

My vision was to build an elegant, intimate, acoustically perfect
concert hall devoted to live jazz music. I wanted to create a performance space that would honor the music and the people who play it.
Too often, even top jazz performers find themselves playing in noisy
clubs in front of people who may or may not know, or care about,
jazz. I wanted to give them the chance to play in a dignified, concert-
like setting, one for attentive audiences who know and love jazz and
respect what jazz artists are trying to do. I also wanted to provide a
first-class venue that would present top artists to jazz fans in Pittsburgh and provide a rallying point where they could celebrate the
city's outstanding jazz heritage. The contributions made to jazz by
cities like New Orleans, St. Louis, Kansas City, and Chicago are well
known, but the list of jazz giants who hail from the Steel City stands
second to none: Erroll Garner and Earl Hines, Art Blakey, Mary Lou
Williams, Stanley Turrentine, and Ahmad Jamal. Duke Ellington discovered Billy Strayhorn working in a drugstore here and made him
one of the premier composers in jazz history. Drummer Kenny Clarke,

singer Dakota Staton, bandleader Billy Eckstine, bassist Ray Brown, and guitarist George Benson are just a few of the groundbreaking jazz masters who called Pittsburgh home. I wanted to honor that tradition. To be honest, when I envisioned my music hall, I imagined it as a place these artists would be proud to call home.

But there was a simpler and deeper reason I wanted to make jazz an essential component of Manchester Bidwell. I needed it. I needed jazz for the same reason I needed clay, the orchids, the sunlight, and the whole hip environment of the school. I needed it all to make my life swing. Swing was a matter of life and death to me. It was what the ghetto had tried to steal away. It's what I've spent a lifetime trying to achieve in my own life and in the lives of others. My life could not be complete without jazz. Neither could my school.

I had intended to include a music hall as part of the building's original design, but because of a miscommunication with my architect, I didn't ask the folks funding the building for quite enough money. And when I hit the streets and tried to raise more cash, my backers met me with puzzled stares. Some of them had already contributed millions to build what many people saw as an unnecessarily opulent facility. They weren't about to cough up more again so quickly. Nor were they convinced that the idea had much merit. We'd need to draw a lot of white folks from affluent communities to make a jazz program fly, they pointed out, and they didn't believe those people would want to park their expensive cars in one of the most crime-ridden neighborhoods in the city. And what, they wondered, does jazz have to do with getting poor kids into college or teaching disenfranchised people the skills they need to get good jobs? At the time, I didn't have good answers to those questions. I knew that telling them it would make the center swing was not likely to win them over. As a last resort, I appealed to Governor Thornburgh, but this time he turned me down. Can't do it, he said. No way we can fund a jazz hall in a school.

At the time, construction on the new facility was still under way, so I asked my architect, Tasso Katselas, if he could find a way to give me a performance space with the budget as it was. The best he could come up with was a multipurpose room with roll-out gymnasium-style bleachers. That wouldn't do, I said. I couldn't ask big-name stars to come all the way to Pittsburgh to perform in a gym. Once again, reality had backed me into a corner. I could have let this dream die, but for me, failure simply wasn't an option when it came to something as vital to my life as jazz. I had to do something to keep my dream alive, so I picked a spot on one wall of the new building, and as masons were laying the bricks of that wall I had them create an archway, identical to all the other brick archways in the center, that the carpenters later walled off with plywood. After that, whenever potential funders—or someone who knew folks who might become potential funders—visited, I marched them past that arch.

"What's that?" they'd ask.

"That's the doorway to my music hall," I'd reply. I wasn't making a statement or a symbolic gesture. I was making a start. I had a doorway—that was as much as I could afford. But a doorway implies a room, and by creating that doorway I was ensuring that the room would happen. That plywood arch was like an unresolved guitar chord hanging in the air. I knew once I strummed it that it couldn't hang forever. It had to resolve itself. The center was unfinished. The dream might be temporarily on hold, but it was alive and present every day. In my mind, the music hall was now inevitable.

Months passed, and every time I looked at my doorway-to-nowhere my vision of the center only grew sharper. I never stopped selling it every way I could, to anyone who would listen. One day I found myself in Governor Thornburgh's office, and for some reason—maybe it was the fact that I knew he was very pleased with the way the center had turned out, and the early success we were having—I sensed a moment of opportunity and brought up the jazz hall again.

"I'm sorry, Bill, I still can't give you money for a jazz hall," he said. Then he smiled and added, "But doesn't a school like yours need an auditorium?"

So we got the money to build an auditorium—an exceptionally stylish auditorium that just happened to feature outstanding acoustical qualities and professional-caliber recording facilities. Construction was completed in 1987, and when I saw the finished music hall I was delighted. The place was everything I had imagined. I couldn't wait to fill it with music. But I had a significant hurdle to overcome: I knew nothing about the music business. I had no idea how to promote a concert, no real contacts in the music industry, no idea how I would let the music world know we existed. I could barely find my way around backstage; all the ropes and pulleys and complicated switchboards for lighting and sound control left me clueless. And so, for months, the hall sat dark and empty.

Then one day I got a call from a young man named Marty Ashby. Marty was a manager in the marketing department for the Pittsburgh Symphony Orchestra, and he had heard about the music hall and my intention to use it as a venue for jazz. A jazz guitarist himself, he had played professionally with some of the biggest names in the business. He had also worked for years as a concert promoter, staging successful jazz festivals in cities across the country. As soon as he introduced himself, I could tell he was as passionate about the idea of bringing jazz to the music hall as I was, and something about the way he presented himself told me he was someone I should meet. So I invited him to come over to tour the facility.

Marty's eyes lit up when he saw the music hall. As I watched him explore every inch of the space and listened to him riff on all the exciting things we could make happen there, I knew I'd met a cat who understood what swing was all about. I offered him the job of building up our jazz program. In a matter of weeks he was hard at work, getting our first subscription series off the ground. Our first season of "Jazz at the Manchester Craftsmen's Guild" was a huge success. Marty brought in major artists like Kenny Burrell, Ray Brown, and Monte Alexander, who drew large, enthusiastic audiences from all over and helped put us on the map. In our second season we attracted heavyweights like Max Roach, Carmen McRae, and Dizzy Gillespie. We went out of our way to treat them with the respect they deserved and never asked them to expect less from us because we were a nonprofit, inner-city organization. We picked them up at the airport in nice cars, got them rooms in good hotels, made sure they ate well and enjoyed themselves while they were here. Most important, we put them onstage in a sleek, sophisticated performance hall that was custom-built to honor the music they'd devoted their lives to, in front of an audience who knew and loved jazz.

We also made certain that they left understanding what Manchester Bidwell was all about. As jazz artists, they loved the creative, improvisational spirit that gave the place its energy, and many of them became strong ambassadors for what we were attempting to do, and an important part of the Manchester Bidwell family. Word started to spread throughout the music community that playing the Manchester Craftsmen's Guild was a choice gig, and after that there was no looking back. Over the next twenty years, virtually all the top names in jazz, including most of the living jazz masters from Pittsburgh, have played here, and the MCG Jazz concert series has become one of the most successful and longest-running jazz subscription series in the country. We produce approximately seventy concerts a year, always to packed houses. Our audiences are made up of people from all over the region, many of them from affluent white neighborhoods, who drive into Manchester, park their Volvos and BMWs in the lot without concern, and lose themselves in the sort of celebration of life and great music I dreamed about every time I stared at that ugly old plywood arch.

The presence of jazz at Manchester Bidwell has done good things for our school. By exposing the place to new populations of people, it has broadened our constituency and opened the doors to new possibilities for funding and partnerships. It has raised our profile in the community and enhanced our image in the eyes of some influential people in ways that make it easier for us to get things done. I didn't build the music hall with any of those things in mind. I only wanted jazz to be an integral part of my school because of how jazz made me feel. The jazz program and everything it has led to came as a happy accident, triggered by my need to find one more way to make my life, and the center, swing.

THIS STATE OF ALIGNMENT or swing that has been so important to me might strike some of you as mysterious or even mystical. But I assure you, there's nothing otherworldly, or elusive, or complicated about it. You probably experience similar moments all the time. The trick is to recognize the value of these moments as they occur, to see the extraordinary promise that hides in ordinary, everyday events. I've taught myself to do this just by paying close attention to the simplest moments of my life. Sometimes, for example, when I'm in the studio making pots, when the light is just right, the jazz I'm listening to is a perfect fit to my mood, and the clay is almost shaping itself in my hands, I fall so completely and so happily into what I'm doing that the rest of the world seems to slip away. Worries and stresses seem trivial. My mind grows clear and quiet. Time turns liquid and hours stream by in what seems like the blink of an eye. In these moments, I'm not consciously contemplating the power of meaningful experience. I'm not intentionally savoring the richness of the experience at hand. And I'm not consciously reminding myself of the importance of being true to my passions. But somehow, all of those things are happening, in an effortless alignment with my skills, my experience, and my creative desires, and I find myself in a state of deep concentration, in what athletes call "the zone," keenly engaged with what I'm doing but also absent in some strange way. I'm not aware of specific thoughts, intentions, or emotions. I'm barely aware of the room around me, and while I can see my hands in front of me, it's easy to forget they belong to me. The pot in front of me fills my awareness—nothing else exists. I become so deeply absorbed in my work that sometimes I forget where Bill Strickland ends and the clay begins.

Usually, I make my best pots that way. But my point is that these moments of transcendent alignment aren't limited to artistic activities. You can experience them while walking in the woods, knitting a sweater, or playing with a child. I've experienced moments like these when I work in my garden, or fishing. Sometimes, it happens when I'm showing my slides of the center to an especially responsive audience. When that happens, and it happens often, my "speech" becomes pure improvisation. I spin out tales and anecdotes I hadn't planned to tell, make connections I hadn't seen before, find a way to tell the Manchester Bidwell story in a way that I know, somehow, will strike that audience right where they live and motivate them to get on their feet and do some good for the world.

Sometimes, these moments of remarkable engagement can last for hours. At other times, they pass in a minute or a moment. But I always come out of these experiences with the uplifting sense that I have reconnected, in a profoundly satisfying way, with the most essential elements of who I am. I've been aware, in a purely intuitive way, that these moments of ringing clarity not only enrich the quality of my life, they give me the insight and impetus I need to nudge my life a little closer to what I want it to be.

For a long time, I didn't know how to articulate or explain these moments of intense engagement—to myself or anyone else. But as I noted earlier, a lot of smart people who have studied these states of "peak experience" had already done that for me.

Flow, says Mihaly Csikszentmihalyi, is any experience in which you become absorbed so completely into what you're doing that the world fades away and nothing else seems to matter. "It is what the sailor holding a tight course feels when the wind whips through her hair, when the boat lunges through the waves like a colt—sails, hull, wind and sea humming a harmony that vibrates in the sailor's veins," he writes. "It is what a painter feels when the colors on the canvas begin to set up a magnetic tension with each other, and a new *thing*, a living thing, takes shape in front of the astonished creator. Or it is the feeling a father has when his child for the first time responds to his smile."

His words sound very familiar to me; I'm sure they call to mind experiences that you've had, too. But what really resonates with me in Csikszentmihalyi's work is his explanation of the mechanism that gives flow its power. In simplest terms, he believes that flow is a natural state of human consciousness—that a human mind, on the fundamental level, is always in a state of wholeness and harmony, always in touch with the authentic needs and values of life, always in a state of orderliness and clarity. But the stresses and distractions of daily life are constantly disrupting this harmonic state. We feel anger, we feel sadness, we are misled by bad assumptions and false priorities. Life wears us down this way until a kind of mental chaos rules our thought processes. In other words, most of us are walking through our days in a state of profound confusion, and we're so conditioned to being confused that we take it as a normal state of mind. Csikszentmihalyi's term for this state of disordered consciousness is "entropy." According to Csikszentmihalyi, flow makes the mind whole again by focusing our attention on an experience so focused and absorbing that it transcends the clutter and noise of daily living. "Flow helps to integrate the self because in that state of deep concentration consciousness is unusually well-ordered," he says. "Thoughts, intentions, feelings and all the senses are focused on the same goal."

In other words, entropy is the opposite of swing. It stifles our potential. It makes us passive and pessimistic. It fills our heads with self-defeating beliefs and clouds our vision of what's possible. At Manchester Bidwell, we see the effects of entropy in one of its most destructive forms. We call it poverty. Poverty is all about disordered thinking. It's all about losing connection with the deepest possibilities of life. One of the things we try to do at Manchester Bidwell is to help our students reconnect with those possibilities. We let them lose themselves in experiences that are rich and meaningful enough to make their broken lives whole again. We help them to see clearly the real potential they hold in their hands.

But you can't talk yourself or someone else into thinking this way. You can't undo entropy with bromides and platitudes or uplifting speeches on self-esteem. You change a person's life, you change your own life, by giving yourself a chance to experience what a good life feels like—a little taste of swing. That's what we do at Manchester Bidwell, and the result is remarkable. People who, all their lives, have allowed themselves to be limited and defined by the low expectations of others and their own limited circumstances suddenly see the possibility of steering their futures in a new and promising direction. They toss off the damage and emotional debris of their old lives the way a snake sheds its skin. They move on. They move up. And maybe that's the ultimate wisdom of "flow": that you don't have to fix everything that's broken in your life—every weakness, every shortcoming, every doubt. You only have to find what works, build on it, trust it, and find a way to make it swing. That wisdom is a powerful lesson for us all.

So where do you find moments of alignment and swing? It's not difficult. In fact, it has less to do with *finding* anything and more to do with seeing past the obstacles that clutter our field of vision. We're surrounded by opportunities to enrich our lives with peak experiences. The best way to connect with these experiences, I think, is to pay close attention to those moments of magic in our lives. Some days after work, as I discussed before, I'll sit in my car before I leave the parking lot and listen intently to some jazz on the stereo. But I mean, I really *listen*. I deliberately refrain from ruminating on all the hassles I might have faced that day, or about what I'm going to do that night or the next day. The jazz at that moment is not mere background music; it *becomes* my life. For others it may be a friend you are conversing with, or gardening in the backyard, or knitting a sweater, or reading a compelling book, or helping with your children's homework. Or jogging, or playing basketball, or making a piece of furniture. The point is, you'll know what it is that is creating that sense of flow. All you have to do is pay attention and let your senses draw you into the moment. If you're taking a walk, feel the sunshine on your skin, the breeze upon your face. If you're eating a memorable meal, slow down, appreciate the taste and texture of every bite. If you're shooting a round of golf, smell the grass, savor the impact of the club on the ball. If you're with another person, remind yourself that this is a moment that you'll never see again.

These moments are always their own reward. But they also serve a very practical purpose: They show us what we lose when we race through our days, skimming the surface of our experience like a rock skipping across a pond. They remind us what a life should feel like. And, what's most surprising to me, they present you with insights you wouldn't otherwise have and prepare you to make the most of unexpected possibilities, serendipities, and subtle connections other people might miss.

One morning in the mid-1990s, I traveled across town with a group from Manchester Bidwell to visit the offices of Bayer, one of our corporate partners, and the people who helped us set up our chemical technician training program. They were also one of the main employers of our chem tech grads, so as we toured the facilities, we had the chance to check on some of our former students. I was pleased to see them thriving in this sophisticated, high-tech environment, working hand in hand with chemists and technologists, loving their jobs and the new lives they were building. And it gratified me to hear the people at Bayer rave about the work our students were doing and how satisfied they were with the relationship with the school. It was a good morning: The air was full of upbeat, creative energy and anything seemed possible.

As we toured the Bayer labs, I spotted one of our chem tech grads operating a small pressing machine that was turning out gleaming silver discs.

"Are those CDs?" I asked. They were, I was told. Bayer, it turned out, held the patent on a polymer called Makrolon MAS 140, a special plastic used to create compact music discs. They were testing the material in hopes of selling it in large quantities to Sony and other companies. As our tour group turned to go, I couldn't take my eyes off the new, shiny CDs coming out of that pressing machine. For a moment, those silver discs were all that I could see.

"Wait a minute," I said to the Bayer executive at my side. "You have the polymer, Sony makes CDs, we have the music. . . . There has to be an opportunity here."

Before we left Bayer that day, I had sketched out in my head a plan to start our own jazz recording label. Bayer was behind it from the start. They brought Sony into the partnership. Sony convinced jewel-case manufacturer DADC to give us the plastic cases we needed, and we talked Mellon Bank into doing the artwork for the CD covers. The deal gave us funding and support to produce three CDs; after that, we were on our own. Marty Ashby geared up our production facilities, and in 1994 our label, MCG Jazz, was born.

Our first release was a live recording of The Count Basie Orchestra and the New York Voices in concert on our stage. Marty and the people under his supervision produced the album with the same high standards we apply to everything we do at Manchester Bidwell, and those efforts were rewarded in 1996 when the release won a Grammy Award for Best Large Jazz Ensemble Performance. It was the first of four Grammys we have won (so far). In the year 2003, we received a Latin Grammy Award for a Brazilian album that paired Paquito D'Rivera with the New York Voices. Two albums with Nancy Wilson won Best Jazz Vocal Album in 2005 and 2007. Overall, of the seventeen albums we've produced for national and international release, seven have been nominated for Grammys. Not a bad batting average for music coming out of an inner-city school in an almost forgotten corner of Pittsburgh.

None of that would have happened without Marty Ashby, of course, and the help of a famous and powerful mutual friend. When I first offered Marty Ashby the job of running our jazz program, I promised him long hours and a substantial pay cut from his previous job. But I also guaranteed him the freedom to do whatever he needed to do to make the program a success.

"I'll take it," he said without hesitation.

"By the way," I said, "I should probably ask for some references." So Marty pulled a sheet of paper from his briefcase. His list of references was long and impressive, but I was stopped short by the name at the top of the list: Dr. Billy Taylor.

"You know Dr. Taylor?" I asked. Marty smiled and nodded. Then he went to work, and less than a year later, when the inaugural season of the MCG Jazz concert series had its opening night, Billy Taylor became the first jazz artist to play on our stage. It was a black-tie affair. The audience was full of political bigwigs and corporate leaders, as well as my mom and my dad. As I heard myself introducing Dr. Taylor, I felt some kind of circle closing. Then he came out and blew everyone away. That show set the bar very high for us and gave us the momentum we needed to jump-start what followed. Dr. Taylor came back many times over the next two decades, and when it was time to celebrate the twentieth anniversary of our jazz program we made sure he headlined the act. In a sense, there would be no jazz at Manchester Bidwell if not for the promise and possibility I'd seen in his music and in who he was. This time, as he filled the hall with jazz, I was also thinking about the bigger picture that Billy's music was a part of: Our orchids were winning prizes; our students were making and eating gourmet food from our own kitchen; kids with no previous artistic background were turning out pots and paintings and photographs. Poor adults were landing demanding jobs that would turn their lives around. Students who'd been written off as failures were thriving and going on to college. We were winning Grammy Awards. Important people were rallying to our cause. None of that happened because I planned it, and none of it was an accident. It happened because I trusted the intuition that the simplest experiences can add richness to our lives and open the door to outrageous possibilities, and because I knew my life would never be my own if I didn't find a way to make it swing.

CHAPTER NINE

Reach

I n December 2001, while promoting the Christmas album she recorded with MCG Jazz (which went on to rank as one of the top five albums of the year on *Billboard* magazine's jazz charts), vocalist Nancy Wilson appeared on *The Oprah Winfrey Show* to perform a few cuts from the album, backed up by our own Marty Ashby and other Pittsburgh musicians who had performed on the recording. She was magnificent, and Oprah's audience responded enthusiastically to the music—music we'd produced with so much care in our studios. Between songs, Oprah explained to her audience that Nancy was giving all of the proceeds from her album to the Manchester Craftsmen's Guild. Then, doing a slight double take for the camera, she joked, "Nancy's giving *all* the proceeds? *Why?*" In her soft, distinctively smoky voice, Nancy told Oprah about our work in Pittsburgh and why she had chosen to team up with us, speaking with the passion and conviction that would make her one of our strongest supporters, and one of our dearest and most trusted friends. "They are making a difference in the community," she said. "They are giving people hope, and

I want to support what they are doing. It is a beautiful place—something every major city should have."

Nancy's words echoed the vision that had already become my new driving mission—to build centers like Manchester Bidwell across the country and around the world, wherever poor people are struggling to survive. I want to build a hundred centers in the United States and a hundred more internationally, each of them fine-tuned to serve the particular needs of the local population. All of them will reflect the essential philosophy of our school: that every human being, despite the circumstances of his or her birth, is born full of potential, and that the way to unlock that potential is to place individuals in a nurturing environment and expose them to the kind of stimulating and empowering creative experiences that feed the human spirit.

Poverty, as I've said before, is a cancer of the spirit; I know that first-hand. The experiences of my life, and thirty years of success in Pittsburgh, have taught me that you don't cure this cancer by defining the poor as people in need of assistance, or by trying to dream up social programs that will fix all the things that are broken in their lives. You cure poverty by understanding that poor folks are *human beings* before they are "poor," and by providing them with access to the fundamental spiritual nourishment *every* human heart requires: beauty, order, purpose, opportunity—the things that give us a meaningful human existence. There's no reason to think that the lessons we've learned are relevant only in Manchester—an orchid is just as beautiful in the streets of São Paulo as it is in Pittsburgh; creativity is just as strong a force for growth in Bangladesh or Palestine as it is in Harlem or North Philly; a safe, serene, and sunlit environment fosters just as much hope and purpose in Belfast or Johannesburg as it does on the South Side of Chicago or in South Central L.A.

This is no idle dream. I know that two hundred centers might not be enough to wipe poverty off the face of the earth. But the dramatic effect those centers would have on tens of thousands of lives, and the social and economic benefits that all those reclaimed lives would offer, just might be enough to force world leaders to rethink the conventional wisdom about fighting poverty and overhaul accepted notions of what can be expected from the poor. We could start an entirely new conversation, based not on tired old assumptions that define poor people as a social burden, but on an enlightened and effective approach that acknowledges the untapped potential of every human being.

We could change social policy. The impact on public education alone would be profound. Imagine American schools that looked and functioned like Manchester Bidwell. Is there any question that graduation rates would soar? Spend some time in an inner-city classroom anywhere in the country, then come to Pittsburgh and spend some time at my school. The truth will be plain as day: If you dismiss the potential of young poor people, teach them, by your attitude and example, to aim low, and send them to learn in a place that looks and feels like a prison, then you're going to get prisoners in return. But if you give them reason to hope, reason to strive, if you offer them a challenging curriculum and a supportive staff in a world-class environment they are proud to be a part of, then you're going to produce citizens who are world class themselves. This is experience, not theory; I see it happening every day. Every kid we send to college, every single mother who gets off the welfare rolls and lands a skilled job, every laid-off factory worker who finds a new future, every formerly homeless person who uses what they learn here to build a dignified, productive life, convinces me more intensely that the lessons we've learned in Manchester have implications that reach far beyond our small corner of the world.

My vision of filling the world with Manchester Bidwell-style schools began to take shape in the mid-1990s. I knew from the start it was an impossible, outrageous ambition, but nearly everything about the place had roots in one outrageous dream or another, so that didn't slow me down. And I wasn't deterred by the magnitude of the challenge; once the vision became real to me, I became convinced that there had to be a way to get from where we were to where we needed to be. I refused to believe it couldn't be done. But *how* to do it stumped me. I simply didn't possess the entrepreneurial know-how to take on such an enterprise; I didn't know how to shape what we'd learned in Manchester and package it into a concept that could be effectively rolled out on such a grand scale. I needed help from someone who knew how to do that. I knew that person was out there somewhere, and that someday our paths would cross. In the meanwhile, I did what I could to move my dream forward: I examined our successes and drew from them reasons to believe what we were doing had universal relevance. Then I crafted those reasons into a story that I told myself and others over and over—the story of how our centers would spread. I told myself the same sorts of stories when I was fighting to make my greenhouse, and earning my pilot's license, and building the center itself. It was my way of fighting off doubt and discouragement and keeping a dream alive. But it was also a way of preparing myself to recognize and capitalize on opportunity if and when it arrived. In effect, by living out that story in my mind, I was rehearsing for eventual success. It's something that I think a lot of successful people do.

I didn't know when or if people who could help my dream come true would enter my field of vision; all I could do was make sure I would recognize my moment of opportunity when it arrived and be prepared to exploit it before it slipped away.

By the late 1990s, the nation had begun to notice Manchester-Bidwell. In 1996, I was appointed to the National Endowment for the Arts, chaired at the time by the actress Jane Alexander, a position that gave me the chance to make important connections at very high levels in the worlds of art and politics. Nineteen ninety-six was also the year the MacArthur Foundation bestowed one of its "genius" grants on me, an honor that triggered a flurry of national media attention, including feature stories in prominent national publications and an especially visible profile of me in the business magazine *Fast Company*. The exposure caught the eye of a lot of influential people who wanted to hear more about our operations, and it created a surge in demand for my services as a speaker. Soon, I found myself carting my clunky old projector and my beat-up box of slides back and forth across the country, telling the Manchester Bidwell story anywhere they'd let me.

In 1996, San Francisco mayor Willie Brown held what he called an economic development summit for his city, and he asked me to speak at the event. Brown loved everything he heard about Manchester-Bidwell, and before the summit was over, he and I were talking seriously about building a similar school for his town. In the weeks and months after the summit, things moved swiftly. Brown let me know that the federal government was about to donate a large parcel of land to the city. The property formerly had been the site of a naval base, in a poor inner-city neighborhood called Bayview Hunters Point, a perfect location for a Manchester Bidwell-type center. When Brown offered us five acres of the parcel as a building site for the school, we eagerly agreed. Shortly thereafter, the city of San Francisco incorporated the project, which would be known as the Bayview Hunters Point Center for Arts and Technology, or BAYCAT, into its redevelopment plan.

It seemed we were off to a fast and promising start, but we soon ran into a formidable snag. When city officials inspected the Navy property before accepting it from the government, they found heavy concentrations of toxic materials in the soil. Nothing could be built there, they said, without a massive environmental cleanup. It soon became clear to us that the Navy was in no hurry to take on the responsibility or the expense of the cleanup, so the BAYCAT project suddenly found itself on indefinite hold.

At the same time, we were struggling to clear another hurdle that, to me, was even more troubling. We had started with a plan to give San Francisco as much as we could of what we had in Pittsburgh— we knew what worked, I reasoned, so why tamper with it? To do that, we'd need a large facility—our design called for a 100,000-square-foot structure, which, we estimated, would cost $30 to $40 million, with an annual operating budget of $5 to $10 million. The price tag was steep, but I was so thoroughly convinced of the worthiness of the project that I had no trouble selling the center, with confidence and passion, to the city's corporate leaders. But in one meeting after another, I watched as those leaders decided that BAYCAT was not worthy of their support. I fought hard to change their minds, but months turned into years, and still no corporate sponsors could be secured. With the project in limbo, political leaders began to lose interest, too. In the meantime, the Navy was continuing to drag its feet on cleaning up the contaminated building site. BAYCAT was foundering, and I slowly came to grips with the fact that my dream of replicating Manchester Bidwell's success in other cities might not come true. It was a bitter pill to swallow, but that doesn't mean I gave up hope. I still believed in BAYCAT, and I kept talking about the project any time I had the chance to anyone who had any interest, or influence, in Bay Area social issues, hoping that my words would soon fall upon the right set of ears.

In the fall of 1999, I was invited to address the annual meeting of the Silicon Valley Community Foundation, a charitable foundation established by key players in California's high-tech industry. My audience that day was made up of some of the most brilliant and tuned-in technological minds in the business world, and as I set up my ancient slide projector in front of them, I never felt more like a throwback. Would anyone stick around to hear what I had to say? I wondered. Or would they write me off as some clueless Luddite with nothing relevant to offer and slip out of the talk as soon as possible? I decided that was up to them. I had no choice but to do what I always do, so I loaded my slides, and when the lights came down, I started the show. As the images of Manchester Bidwell flashed on the screen behind me, I supplied the narration that I hoped would be the seeds of ideas I wanted to plant in their minds. *I'm not here asking for charity,* I told them. *I'm here to show you something that works, and to tell you the important lessons I've earned. One of the most important lessons I have to share is about the amazing resiliency of the human spirit. I've seen it so many times in Pittsburgh. People come to us weighted down with self-destructive assumptions about life, about what's possible, about their own potential and self-worth. So many of them have led brutal lives, and have been so coarsened and hardened by their experiences, that it's hard to see in them any trace of the softness or sensitivity a dream needs to take root. It would be easy to write them off as lost causes. But I've seen so many of them turn their lives around that I refuse to write any of them off, even the ones who come in thinking dreams are for fools and hope is for chumps. My work has convinced me that the human spirit is extremely difficult to crush. We see broken people here, we see lives in which the fires of hope and possibility are not much more than a sputtering flicker. But when that little flicker gets the proper fuel, when the human heart finds beauty and meaning and purpose, that day the flame starts to burn so bright, so fast it will make your head spin. Some of our students remind me of a fading flower struggling to grow in inhospitable ground. If you transplant the flower to good soil and give it some water, the roots soak up the nutrients and, almost before your eyes, the drooping flower thrives: It straightens on its stem, the brown leaves turn green again, and all the color comes back to the blossom. So don't be too quick to give up on poor people,* I told my audience. *They just might surprise you. They might turn out to be diligent and committed students. They might just be the kind of employee any employer would love to hire. They might possess dreams and strengths and talents that would surprise you. One of them, in fact, might even win a Genius award, get his name in the* New York Times, *and wind up being the keynote speaker in front of a lot of smart people like you.*

We know what works, I tell them. *And if it works in Pittsburgh, it will work around the world. I know what we have to do, but I need your help to do it. We all have a chance to make a contribution to the world we live in; we all have the duty to recognize our responsibility to the planet and the people we share it with. If my talk today has any impact whatsoever, I hope it gets you thinking about ways to use your resources, your abili-*

ties, all the experience you've gathered and the lessons you've learned, to spread hope and make the world a better place for everyone who lives here.

I made sure to tell them all about BAYCAT, and was not shy in asking for their support for the project. Then I ended the talk and watched as the audience rose as one and gave me a loud and sustained ovation. The emotion in the room caught me by surprise, and soon I found myself surrounded by a crowd of people pressing forward to talk with me. I shook hands all around, filled my pocket with business cards, and encouraged everyone who spoke with me to think about ways they could use their talents and position to make things a little better in the world. In the midst of this commotion, a young man introduced himself to me. He said his name was Jeff Skoll, and he mentioned the company he worked for, but it didn't ring a bell. He liked my message, he said, and wanted to know how he could learn more about my plans. There was nothing in his outward appearance to set him apart from the rest of the pack; he was dressed in jeans, I think, a casual shirt, and running shoes—the typical uniform for the West Coast techies in the room. He struck me as a genuine and straightforward person, and I liked him right away. But what really left an impression on me was something I read in his eyes. It was more than enthusiasm or curiosity; Jeff had the look of someone who knew he had something important to offer, and who might have found an idea worth offering it to. With all the people gathered around me, there wasn't time to talk, so I took his business card, gave him mine, and turned to shake the next hand.

A few days later, back at Manchester Bidwell, I took all the business cards I'd gathered on the trip and flipped through them until I found the one I wanted. It read:

JEFF SKOLL

Vice President, Strategic Planning and Analysis
eBay

As you know by now, I'm not the most technologically sophisticated guy in the world, and I was even less so back in '99, so "eBay" as a company meant nothing to me. But something about the sound of it held my attention. I took the card and went out into the hall of the school, where I flagged down the first student I could find. "Do you know what eBay is?" I asked him.

"Sure, Mr. Strickland," he answered. "It's the electronic commerce network—that online auction Web site." At last, the light went on in my head. I'd heard, recently, about eBay going public, and how that made its founders—Jeff included—instant billionaires. I replayed our meeting in my mind and hoped I hadn't brushed him off too rudely.

In moments, I had him on the phone.

"Mr. Skoll," I said, "I have come to have a much deeper appreciation of who you are, man."

"I thought you'd figure it out," he chuckled. Then he got down to business, and what he told me made my head spin. Jeff had already established The Skoll Community Fund, a charitable foundation created to inspire and encourage the kind of socially responsible entrepreneurialism that he believed was the best way to make positive changes in the world. He told me that the style in which I was running Manchester Bidwell—the way we balanced social action with entrepreneurial vigor—was a perfect example of the kind of leadership he wanted to foster. He even said the potential he saw in our operations reminded him of how he'd felt about eBay in its infancy and suggested Manchester Bidwell could be the eBay of social change.

"I like what you said about replicating centers in cities everywhere," he said. "I'd like to help you with that, beginning with BAYCAT."

That was all I needed to hear. In short order, we had Jeff, along with Peter Hero, director of the Silicon Valley Community Foundation, fly into Pittsburgh to tour our operations. He liked what he saw, so we sat down and started mapping out a plan. From the start, Jeff insisted that we take a more businesslike approach to the challenges of replication. He pointed out that I had been thinking of the San Francisco center as the solution to a social problem, as an idea or a dream I wanted to make real. Jeff urged me to think of it as a product. You can't simply impose your product on the world and expect it to be embraced, he said. You have to find the essence of your product, understand what it is that you're really selling, then help it find its place in the world in a way that will allow it to thrive. We had to think about BAYCAT the way entrepreneurs think about launching a new enterprise. Entrepreneurs don't see setbacks as defeats, he said, but as detours. You learn from them, you make adjustments and refinements, you do what you have to do to keep moving toward the goal. The biggest lesson that an entrepreneur would learn from our San Francisco experience, Jeff said, is that you can't allow yourself to be boxed in by your own expectations or by some preconceived picture you have in your head.

In a nutshell, Jeff was saying that we'd gotten the scale of the San Francisco center all wrong. We were trying to transplant everything we had in Pittsburgh to the West Coast, hoping it would take root there and flourish. But Manchester Bidwell was the product of more than thirty years of slow, organic growth that was shaped by the particular needs and resources of the city, all the connections I'd made in the course of a lifetime, and, most important, by all the transforming experiences that had helped shape me as a human being. The Pittsburgh center was unique; we couldn't simply copy what we'd done there and build it from scratch in another city. We had to distill the essence of our success, plant that essence like a seed in new soil, and let new centers grow into what they had to be to best address the needs and resources of the community they would serve. With Jeff's help, I learned an important lesson from the setbacks in San Francisco: I realized that we weren't selling Manchester Bidwell, we were selling what the Manchester Bidwell Center is made of—transforming experience, an empowering environment, opportunities for growth and self-discovery. Our product was purpose; we were selling meaning and hope. Once I saw that with clarity, I agreed with Jeff that the next logical step was to find a way to sell those things in the most effective, most entrepreneurial manner.

The first thing we decided upon was that we'd never again launch a replication effort without strong commitments from the local corporate community. Our hope in San Francisco had been that Willie Brown's endorsement would give us the credibility we needed to attract the support of locally based corporations. It didn't happen. We couldn't even generate enough of a focused will among local politicians to win the support of all-important city officials. It would be smarter, we realized, to approach corporations directly. Corporations have the money. If they decide to become involved, they are capable of swift, focused action. So our first step would be to find a willing corporate partner; once we got big business on board, city leaders were bound to follow.

Our second resolution was an offshoot of the first: We didn't want to go to those corporations with our hat in our hands, asking them to be the solution to our problem. We wanted to offer corporate leaders our solution to a problem they faced in their cities, and to show them all the reasons it was in their interest to become part of our plan. To do that, we needed to show we could play the game on terms that made sense in their world. The first step, Jeff said, was to draw up a sharply focused business plan so we could present ourselves to potential partners in a format they would understand, and respond swiftly and decisively with advice that would give them the best chance of getting new centers off the ground. For starters, the plan called for center organizers to identify their major funding sources—corporations, foundations, or government agencies, for example—and then secure from them a preliminary grant totaling $150,000. That amount, we determined, was enough to get all essential planning processes started; it would also give us an early sign that a given community could muster the necessary support a center needed to thrive. Once that money was in hand, our plan would call for swift action to assemble a team of advisers, locate a suitable space, develop a curriculum that suited the needs and resources of a particular city, then find a director and begin the process of raising the funds needed to build and operate the center.

While we refined the details of the business plan, we got the good news that the Skoll Community Fund had agreed to give us a sizable grant, which provided us with the funding and support we hadn't been able to raise from the San Francisco corporate community. After years of hope and struggle, BAYCAT was going to happen. But it would be a dramatically scaled-back version of the operation we had first proposed. For starters, we decided to keep costs down by building a much smaller center than we originally imagined. To further simplify the equation, we streamlined the adult job-training programs to focus on digital imaging and film and video, with an eye toward future job opportunities in those and related industries, along with arts education programs for middle and high school students. This time around, we weren't trying to build the center of our dreams; it would be enough to establish a beachhead, get programs up and running on a foundation that allowed for future growth, and in the meantime change a lot of young people's lives.

As BAYCAT progressed through the planning and construction stages, I continued to travel the country showing my slides, hoping to find and connect with people who might embrace my vision and help me spread it across the country. The more I showed my slides, the more we heard from leaders in other cities, asking how they could bring something like Manchester Bidwell to their towns. Most of those inquiries never passed beyond the stage of conversation, but I kept on spreading the word, because I knew the right people were out there and that I'd find them sooner or later.

I found two of them in Lee Carter, who was then chairman of the board of Children's Hospital in Cincinnati, and Linda Tresvant, director of an arts education program called Art Links. They had seen me give my slide show at an appearance in Ohio, and a few weeks later Lee visited us in Pittsburgh to examine the feasibility of building a facility like ours in Cincy. We sent Lee home with a copy of our business plan and our commitment to work with him to make the Cincinnati center happen, and he set to work gathering the community support he would need. In 2003, Lee's efforts paid off as the Cincinnati Center for Arts and Technology opened its doors, offering an arts curriculum for middle school kids featuring programs in digital imaging, computer and graphic design, animation, and ceramics, and a job-training program in automotive technology, all supported by corporate partners that included Procter & Gamble, Fifth Third Bank, and the Cincinnati-based Castellini Company, one of the largest distributors of fresh fruits and vegetables in the country, run by Bob Castellini, who is also the principal owner of the Cincinnati Reds and now one of the Manchester Bidwell family's strongest corporate supporters.

At about the same time that the Cincinnati center debuted, BAYCAT opened for business in San Francisco, with arts programs in audio, video, computer animation, and film. Two years ago, the Manchester Bidwell family added a third center when Jim Hackett, CEO of Michigan-based Steelcase Corporation, an industry leader in office furnishings and design, heard me speak at a conference sponsored by *Fast Company* magazine and decided that Steelcase would spearhead the development of a Manchester Bidwell-style center in Grand Rapids. With strong support from another prime sponsor, the DeVos family, of Alticor (formerly Amway) fame, and the help of Jim Welsh, a former Steelcase executive, Jim Hackett oversaw the creation of the West Michigan Center for Arts and Technology, which offers job programs that train adults for positions in medical coding and billing and as pharmaceutical techs, as well as providing arts programs in photography, computer imaging, and ceramics. Each center differs in size and scope, but all have embraced the essential Manchester Bidwell philosophy, providing a sophisticated, empowering physical environment, educational programs that are effective and stimulating, and a culture that sets the bar high and expects every student to reach deep to discover their hidden potential. It's still early in the game for these centers, but from all indications they're on track to achieve the same kind of success we enjoy at Manchester Bidwell. The Cincinnati center graduates almost 90 percent of its students from high school and sends 72 percent on to college. Grand Rapids hasn't yet graduated a high school class, but in a city where the annual school dropout rate hovers around 40 percent, they've managed to keep all but 5 percent of their students in school. That puts them on track to do what we do in Pittsburgh—graduate almost all of their kids and send most of them to college. They've also placed 75 percent of their pharmacy students in good jobs. We're seeing good things in San Francisco, too, where a growing majority of students at BAYCAT are deciding to stay in school.

Meanwhile, as I keep showing my slides and spreading our story, more and more cities are reaching out to be part of our success. As of this moment, groups in Cleveland, Columbus, Philadelphia, and New Orleans have secured the $150,000 preliminary grants they need to get their centers started. We're also having serious conversations with groups in Chicago, Los Angeles, Reno, New Haven, and Charlotte, North Carolina, who are working to get early funding and move their projects forward to the planning stage. In recent years, as word of our success has spread around the planet, we've received more and more inquiries from foreign countries that believe that what we've discovered in Pittsburgh might be part of the answer for difficult social problems they face. Last year we met with a group in Japan that is interested in establishing schools that would serve the children of Korean immigrants, who have become Japan's poorest, and sometimes most slighted, underclass. Next year, I'll visit Israel, at the request of Israeli government officials, who want to establish a Manchester Bidwell–type program that would bring Israeli and Palestinian kids together in the same classrooms. I'll also travel to Belfast, where Northern Ireland officials want to use schools like ours to teach Protestant and Catholic kids, side by side and under the same roof. More recently, I've been working with a group of influential Costa Rican leaders who want to build a center in their country.

The fact that we are attracting that kind of attention, from different kinds of societies in far-flung corners of the world, each of them facing problems that are deeply rooted in their history and culture, shows me that people are able to see the true nature of the promise that Manchester Bidwell offers. We aren't just a "poverty program," with relevance only for poor black people living in American inner cities. We're a world-class training center for all kinds of people who are struggling to improve their lives. The principles our school is built on work because they transcend the superficial criteria societies typically use to classify people—race, gender, or socioeconomic class. We define each one of our students as a distinct human being, full of unique hopes and dreams and abundant untapped potential. Manchester Bidwell makes a strong argument that poverty and all the suffering and social strife it leads to are, in essence, the result of a profound frustration of the basic human drive to live a life that has purpose, dignity, and meaning, issues we all face, on some level, in our efforts to make the most of ourselves.

OUR CAMPAIGN TO BUILD centers nationwide wouldn't be where it is today if Jeff Skoll hadn't appeared on our radar screen and decided that Manchester Bidwell was something he needed to be part of. Today, as director of the National Center for Arts and Technology, the board we created to manage our replication process, Jeff is helping us roll out our brand of entrepreneurial social action to cities everywhere.

As part of the Manchester Bidwell team, he joins the legion of influential mentors and allies who have rallied around me all my life, from Frank Ross on down, and helped me build the life I longed for. I wouldn't have accomplished half of what I have without such a strong and committed team of supporters. How did I build such a team? I have the uncanny sense that this small army of champions, advisers, and benefactors somehow assembled itself. It seems that at every turning point in my life, when I needed guidance, or strength, or inspiration, when I needed a door to be opened or an introduction to be made, when I needed financial or political backing, or when I simply needed a reason to carry on, a powerful supporter appeared in my life to give me what I needed to keep my dreams alive.

Is the uncanniness with which these people appeared in my life the result of luck, or did I do something to attract them? Part of the answer, I think, has to do with a disposition I seem to have been born with, which inclines me to recognize certain individuals as people who have an important role to play in my life. I was not the only kid to walk by the art room door at Oliver High School and see Mr. Ross working on his pots. I wasn't the only student who had the chance to benefit from his instruction. But I was the only one to sense the potential he offered me, and once I sensed it, I made it my business to show Mr. Ross I was someone who was worthy of his time. But what did Frank Ross see in me? Why did he open up his life to me and allow me to become his friend? For that matter, what led any of the people whose help was such a crucial part of my success to go to such great lengths to help me and make my vision a part of their lives? My guess is this: At the same time I was recognizing them as individuals who could open doors for me, they were seeing in me someone who could contribute something to their own efforts to live a purposeful, meaningful life. No one accomplishes anything really worthwhile without the help of others. Learning to spot others in life who can help you to achieve your goals is a key component of success. But I'm convinced that knowing how to present yourself in a way that allows them to recognize you is an even more important talent to master.

There's a story about jazz legend Billy Strayhorn that drives this lesson home. Strayhorn, a Pittsburgh native, was a twenty-three-year-old drugstore clerk in 1938 when Duke Ellington and his orchestra came to town for a show. An aspiring musician and composer, Strayhorn was playing piano in clubs at night, featuring original music he had composed and arranged. (While still in his teens, Billy had created some remarkable music, including the haunting ballad "Lush Life," which would become one of the great jazz standards of all time.) On the evening of Ellington's concert, Strayhorn somehow found his way backstage and managed to meet the great man himself. After shaking Ellington's hand, he handed him some sheet music. It was the score of one of Ellington's own compositions, but Strayhorn had reworked the arrangement to show how he would have improved it. It was a risky and audacious move—Ellington was already a part of American music royalty, and his records topped the charts around the world. But instead of being offended, Ellington saw Strayhorn's brilliance leaping off the pages. After the concert, Ellington took some members of his band to a local club where Billy was playing, and was so impressed he invited Strayhorn to visit him in New York City to discuss the possibility of a musical collaboration. When Billy arrived at Ellington's New York residence, he had a gift for Duke: a song he had written and arranged just for the occasion, based on the directions to Ellington's apartment. The tune was called "Take the 'A' Train." Ellington was so taken with the tune that he made it his theme song, and it has since become one of the standards of American popular music. Ellington and Strayhorn would go on to become one of the great songwriting teams in music history, with Strayhorn providing the songs—masterpieces like "Lush Life," "Satin Doll," "Lotus Blossom," and "Chelsea Bridge"—that made him a jazz immortal and helped earn Ellington a reputation as one of the masters of American popular music.

For me, the pivotal moments in recounting that story are not when Strayhorn meets Ellington backstage before the concert, or when he shows up at Ellington's apartment with the sheet music for "'A' Train" in his hand. The key moments happened before Billy had met Duke Ellington, before he had any rational reason to hope that he would ever meet someone of Ellington's stature. They were the moments Billy spent dreaming up melodies in his head, after putting in his shift at that Pittsburgh drugstore, scribbling down his music when he could, honing his compositions by testing them out night after night in neighborhood saloons. He took his dreams seriously and lived his life in a way that prepared him for the day when opportunity might favor him. When it did, Billy was ready. He not only recognized his opportunity, he had prepared himself for it so thoroughly that when Ellington saw Billy he could not help but recognize a soul mate and a partner.

There's a phrase jazz musicians use: They say, *Tell your story.* They're talking about a way of playing that not only displays your virtuosity but also gives the audience a glimpse of your soul. Billy Strayhorn knew his story long before Duke Ellington entered his life. It was in his music, and when Ellington heard him play he knew all he needed to know to see that he had found in Billy a musical partner who could help him complete and expand his own musical vision. We all have stories to tell. In fact, we can't avoid telling them. We tell them every time we interact with another person, form a friendship, interview for a job, fall in love, ask for help, or share a dream. What my experiences prove to me is that the more clearly and convincingly you are able to tell your story, the better your chance of attracting the people who can best help you move your story forward, and in whose own stories you can play a productive part. In retrospect, I realize that all the important connections I made in my life, all the great partners and mentors I've gathered and all the opportunities they have made possible, have come as a result of sharing my story with others who are interested in being a part of that story. My story has many versions—one is about clay, one is about orchids, one is about jazz, one is about the center I built out of a dream, and another is about my dream of building similar centers around the world. But underneath all of them lies a simpler, deeper story with a more fundamental message: *This is what I stand for; this is who I am.* I tell that story every chance I get, and it's still helping me connect with people who are willing and able to help me enlarge my vision and accomplish my dreams.

Recently, Marty Ashby and I were in Los Angeles discussing a recording deal between MCG Jazz and Concord Records, an important jazz label co-owned by TV producer Norman Lear. We were there to talk about music, but when the Concord executives heard me talk about Manchester Bidwell, they decided it was a story their boss should hear. So a meeting was hastily arranged with Mr. Lear in his office down the hall. He greeted us warmly and invited us to take a seat. Then he looked me in the eye and spoke plainly. "They've told me a little about you, and it sounds like you're doing wonderful work," he said, "but I have to tell you right up front, I don't have any money for you."

"That's okay," I said. "I just want you to know who we are." And I meant that, too. So I reached into my briefcase and pulled out the CD on which my slide show was stored—I've gone digital, at last—and with the loan of one of Mr. Lear's computers, we started the show. I ran the presentation like always: no sales pitches, no impassioned speeches about the plight of the poor. I just let him see the pictures for himself and told the story of how what he was looking at came to be. When we finished, he turned to me with a thoughtful look in his eye.

"How much would it take to start a center like this in L.A.?" he asked.

"One hundred fifty thousand dollars to get the planning started," I replied.

Norman Lear nodded. "You've got the money," he said, and a Los Angeles center was on its way to being born. That didn't happen because of my persuasive abilities; it happened because what Mr. Lear saw in the slides matched up with a way of thinking that already made sense in his life. He wasn't doing charity; he was telling his story, and he recognized me as someone who could help him tell part of that story in a new and effective way.

My experience convinces me that this kind of synergistic connection, this natural, mutually beneficial dovetailing of like-minded spirits, is at the heart of all successful teams and partnerships. It certainly plays a big role in how we build the Manchester Bidwell staff. Just recently, someone asked me how I am able to consistently find so many high-quality, highly motivated employees. "I don't," I replied. "They find me." I wasn't being funny; I wasn't being smug. We have no trouble finding great employees, because the very sort of people we want to hire are the ones who are most powerfully attracted to the Manchester Bidwell story. And we hire them knowing that they aren't simply buying into our story, they are changing that story a little by adding their own. We encourage that. We insist upon it. In fact, I expect the same things from our employees that I expect from our students: that they embrace possibility, that they explore their own potential, that they shape their work in ways that stimulate their own personal growth, that they push themselves and, in the process, push me. I don't expect them to fit into some pigeonhole I've created; I want them to tell me their story in a way that amplifies and facilitates mine, and that makes the whole much more than the sum of its parts.

When Marty Ashby showed up at my door years ago, for example, he didn't know I was looking for someone to run a jazz program. For that matter, neither did I. He was drawn here by an intuitive interest in the school. But when we met we each recognized possibility in the other, and out of that possibility a new team was born. I could have given Marty some structured directive about what I expected him to accomplish and how he should proceed. If I had, I doubt I'd have had the vision to ask for everything he's accomplished. (Imagine me telling Marty: *I want you to turn this place into a national venue for live jazz, start an independent record label here in Manchester, and win a few Grammys in the process.*) Luckily, I felt no urge to micromanage. Instead, on Marty's first day on the job, I handed him the keys to the music hall and told him, "Have a nice life." Marty eagerly accepted that freedom and shouldered the responsibility that came with it, and thanks to the way he operates—to the way he tells his story—he attracted all the right employees, experts, partners, and performers to make the jazz program an astonishing success.

I didn't hire Marty because of his résumé, as good as it was; I hired him because he was able to show me more than credentials. He showed me who he was, he showed me what jazz meant to him, and I couldn't miss his enthusiastic vision for the role jazz could play at Manchester Bidwell. Marty didn't come here looking for a job, he was looking for a mission.

Jesse Fife, on the other hand, may not have known he was looking for a mission when I hired him in those difficult early days at the Bidwell Training Center, but I knew he was a young man hungering for a meaningful way to use his talents. Jesse was a rare find for me, a guy who possessed both an innate business savvy and a big, open heart. His genius was to intuitively grasp the same insight that K. Leroy Irvis would later share with us—that social programs couldn't get by on good intentions alone. From the start Jesse understood that if we wanted to make a real difference we had to present ourselves like no other social program had done before. He insisted that we develop levels of accountability and professionalism that would show the corporate world—the people who held the power we needed to truly succeed—that we were organized, serious, effective, and reliable. We had to speak their language. We had to move confidently in their world. We had to show them we were making change in a way that would be fiscally responsible and that could be tracked and verified in ways that would justify their support. Jesse's ability to strike a delicate balance—doing what we needed to do for our students, while addressing the concerns and sensibilities of the business world—is a fundamental reason I've been able to realize, and sustain, my vision for the school. It still amazes me, the way he listens to me rant and rave, then finds a way to turn my passion into action. His style is laid-back and low-profile, but his fingerprints are all over every success we've had. But what's pertinent here is that he didn't come to me with those skills intact. He developed them as he grew into his role here, as a function of his own personal growth and the growing sense of mission with which his passion for his work has shaped who he is.

The staff at Manchester Bidwell is filled with people like Marty and Jesse, people who know how to turn their work into a calling. Most of them could be making more money somewhere else, but they stay because the possibilities this place offers them match up so well with the stories they've told themselves, that let them live the lives they want. I believe all successful people start out by telling themselves stories that convince them that what they want is within their reach. Every dream and wishful thought about the future is a part of your story; they all help you rehearse for the future you dream of. They even increase the chances of that future coming true.

I've been shaping my life with stories since I was a kid. I was the guy who was going to turn clay into a future, grow orchids in the ghetto, learn to fly, and turn lives around by building the hippest "poverty center" on the planet. Now I'm the guy who's going to spread the magic of that center all over the world. Making the impossible possible seemed more doable once I transformed the dreams into stories I told to myself and to others so often that I couldn't help but be convinced that they would come true. And many of them have. But success has never been a solo mission. I wouldn't have done half of what I've accomplished without the assistance of countless friends, advisers, partners, coworkers, and kindred spirits. And each time I've crossed paths with such a person, it was a meeting that seemed inevitable, as if they had been waiting to find me. I guarantee you, the people you need to meet in your life are out there, waiting to hear from you, waiting for you to tell your story. But you have to get the story right. The world is full of people who know what they want. That's not a story. A story shows people that you know what you want *to be.* If you can tell that story, with conviction and sincerity, I'm convinced that you'll catch the ear of the right crowd and point yourself in the direction of extraordinary experience and meaningful success.

CHAPTER TEN

Purpose

When I took my first flight on an airplane—the same trip on which I discovered my passion for flying—I was traveling to Boston to visit a girl I knew. Our time together in Boston was magical, and not just because I was crazy about her. There was something about being in Boston with her, in that center of culture and history and tradition, that sharpened a hunger in me for a quality of experience I wasn't yet able to put into words. We visited all the historical sites. We had cocktails in the lounge of a famous hotel on Boston Common. We walked on Beacon Street and along the Esplanade beside the Charles River. She worked at Harvard University, and one day she gave me a tour of the Harvard campus. For a young man who'd barely been out of Manchester, it was a heady experience. I felt as if I had slipped in through the back door to a mythical place, so rich in tradition and possibility that the very air we breathed seemed thick with ideas and class, power and privilege. It was a world I knew I could never be a part of, but I didn't resent that. I drank in the rarefied atmosphere, hoping there was something here, some insight, some experience, that I could make my own and take back home with me to Manchester.

As we passed the ivy-covered building of the Harvard Business School, I asked if we could take a look inside. My friend led me in through the old double doors and down a long corridor lined with large portraits of old, scowling white guys—captains of industry, I guessed, or Supreme Court justices, maybe a former cabinet member or two. At the end of the corridor was an open door. I leaned into the doorway and peered into an empty classroom. A podium stood at the front of the room, facing rising tiers of wooden seats. I thought about the students who sat in those seats. I wondered about their lives and the circumstances that had brought them to this place of great expectations. I imagined all the things that their experiences here would make possible for them in the future. As we turned to leave, I felt a sudden surge of longing. I can't say I felt envy—it was more a sense of acknowledgment. There was something about the things that room promised that I wanted to be part of.

Twenty years later, I found myself walking along that same long corridor again, past the somber portraits of those patriarchal white dudes, and entered the very same lecture hall. This time the seats were full of students—the graduate students in Jim Heskett's business class that I described in the beginning of the book—and they were waiting for me. As I took my place at the podium, I couldn't help glancing at the doorway, half expecting to see my younger self staring back at me. What would he think? What would I say to him now if I had the chance?

And I realized I'd want him to know the same things I was about to share with the Harvard students: that a good life isn't something you wait for, or chase after, or try to possess; it's something you must create, moment by moment, on the foundation of your dreams. But first, you need to understand your dreams and embrace them. Most important, you need to know the difference between a dream and a fantasy, because it's impossible to live a fulfilled, happy life until you do. Teaching our students to make that distinction is one of the primary missions of Manchester Bidwell and a key reason for its success. Too many come to us with their heads full of unrealistic cheap fantasies that they learn on the streets, believing there are shortcuts to wealth, position, and power. Most of these fantasies lead to dead ends—after all, how many kids are going to make it as pro athletes or hip-hop stars? Other, more sinister, fantasies that draw them into gangs or drugs or crime can kill them. They embrace these fantasies because the world doesn't seem to offer them any alternatives. Once you give them a reason to hope for something real, the fantasies tend to evaporate and solid, empowering dreams take their place. All of us can learn from their experience. We're all in danger of mistaking fantasies for dreams at times—we allow our hopes and expectations to be shaped by circumstances and conventional wisdom, just as poor black kids allow their lives to be shaped by the conventional wisdom of the ghetto. Millions of us base our lives on the conventional fantasy that the pursuit of material success is the path to happiness. I'm convinced that misguided beliefs like that can block us from achieving our full human potential. But with a little effort and experience, we can distinguish between a misleading fantasy and a life-enriching dream.

A fantasy is about *having* something—a big salary, an impressive house, an important-sounding title, social or professional prestige. But the satisfaction you experience when such a fantasy is realized is fleeting and unfulfilling; rather than feeding the spirit in a nourishing way, it always leaves you craving more.

A dream is about *building* something—relationships, identity, quality of experience. Because dreams rise out of genuine human needs, they feed the spirit in a profoundly satisfying way. A genuine dream brings direction, conviction, substance, and satisfaction to your life *the moment you commit yourself to it.*

But the most important difference between fantasies and dreams is that fantasies are egotistical and self-centered; they isolate you and force you to live your life as a series of win-lose situations. They define "success" as a matter of the survival of the fittest. Dreams, on the other hand, connect you to the world and to other human beings. They make it clear that individual success is enlarged and enhanced by the spiritual fulfillment and success of the people with whom you share the planet.

All my experience has taught me that the ability to base your life on sound, substantial dreams is a fundamental requirement of living a meaningful and successful life. I'm not alone in that thinking; I've heard the same message from people who know a whole lot more about material success than I do.

For example, when Jeff Skoll and I started working together, I had the chance to speak with his mother. "Jeff talks about you all the time," she told me. "He never tells me anything about his work. But he's so committed to building this school; I've never seen him so excited about anything in his life."

Jeff is a guy who helped build a world-changing business in eBay. He made billions of dollars, yet what excites Jeff is the work others are doing to help kids and change the world. I've heard similar things from Quincy Jones, Norman Lear, Nancy Wilson, and prominent politicians of both parties as well as heads of major corporations eager to be part of our story. It's certainly not because what we're doing at Manchester Bidwell will make them richer or more famous. They already know all they need to know about material success. They know how to achieve the benefits it offers. But they also understand its limits, and they know that the human soul needs something more. I don't think people like these embrace a vision like mine out of altruism alone.

It's the human experience they're after, the validation and sense of fulfillment our mission provides. All of these folks know what it feels like to accomplish extraordinary things and win the respect and recognition of the world. But what I hear from them, and what I see in their actions time and time again, is that there is no experience that makes them feel more vividly, passionately, and purposefully alive than the chance to use their talents and resources to bring more dignity, hope, and opportunity into the world and reduce the suffering that devalues so many human lives.

These people have had these insights made clear to them by the path that led them to fortune and fame, but I knew the same things, intuitively, when I was a street kid in Manchester. I sensed, somehow, that life is a gift, and that it's the job of every one of us to use that gift to the best advantage. Why settle for some comfortable, conventional idea of what a good life is supposed to be? Why not do something remarkable with our time on the planet? Why not set our sights outrageously high? Why shouldn't you help to leave things a little better than you found them? Why not make it your business to help inspire the world?

You don't have to be rich and famous to take on such a mission. You don't have to be a world leader, a CEO of a major corporation, a genius, or a saint. You don't have to move to the slums of Calcutta or live on the plains of Darfur. You don't even have to leave your neighborhood. I live six blocks from the house I grew up in; my entire life has been played out in an urban landscape that covers maybe a square mile.

Every day, the world invites you to make a difference. You only need to recognize these invitations and respond in a way that suits your ambitions, your values, your resources, and your passion. Few of us have the stuff to become another Gandhi, Mandela, Mother Teresa, or Martin Luther King Jr. But all of us can be part of the same continuum of heroic humanitarianism, in however modest a way. Bangladeshi entrepreneur Muhammad Yunus found his place on that continuum by establishing the micro-lending system that helped millions of Third World residents escape servitude and devastating poverty, and recognition of his efforts won him the Nobel Peace Prize. Janet Nkubana, a single mother living in the Rwandan capital, Kigali, saw the suffering of so many women around her whose husbands had been killed in the genocide there and who were struggling now to survive, and decided to help them. An artist herself, she was taken with the beauty of the handmade baskets these women produced, and while she had no experience in sales or marketing, she found a way to earn significant money for her countrywomen by selling their baskets at craft fairs and arts festivals in the United States. In 2003, she met Willa Shalit, an American women's rights advocate, who was so inspired by Nkubana's work that she proposed to Macy's department store in New York the idea of selling the Rwandan baskets. Macy's agreed. The handmade "peace baskets" have since become a brisk seller for Macy's and have helped improve the quality of life for countless Rwandan women and their families. But you don't need to go very far from home to make a difference. One of the most moving stories I've ever heard was about a little girl, suffering with incurable leukemia, who set up a lemonade stand on the sidewalk in front of her house to raise money for other kids with cancer whose families couldn't pay for treatment. Thank God for her courage and the size of her heart. And recently, I heard a story here in Pittsburgh about a large public pool in a working-class neighborhood that was closing because local government couldn't afford to make repairs. One man in that community refused to accept that decision. He went door to door with a coffee can in hand, asking for dimes and nickels to save the pool. When others saw his example, they joined in, too, and soon they had raised the thousands of dollars they needed to repair the pool, which opened in time for the summer season, giving hundreds of blue-collar kids a safe and fun alternative to the streets.

Every one of those people made the world a more humane place simply by recognizing that it was within their reach to do so. The impact of their actions may have been small, but I don't think that's what matters. I'm convinced that whatever direct impact your actions might have upon the condition of the world is, in the long run, less important than the impact the decision to act will have upon your soul. Owning up to the responsibilities you have to the earth and the people you share it with makes you more whole and more human—in small but important ways. And when all is said and done, that's what my story is really all about, because if we could only get enough engaged human beings walking the planet, if we could fill the streets with people living lives based on responsibility and compassion, if more of us led lives that left us spiritually nourished, eased our fears, gave us the meaningful and fulfilling kind of success that all human hearts long for, then a lot of the problems that plague us as a society would start taking care of themselves.

We can start living that life this moment. No step is too small. Pick up some trash. Check on an elderly neighbor. Volunteer at a school or a homeless shelter. Commit yourself to a passion that moves you. Or give us a call at Manchester Bidwell. We're always looking for new energy and new ideas. But whatever you do, don't do it out of obligation or because you think service to others will help you earn some imaginary set of angel's wings. Take my advice—do it because it's the only way I'm aware of to live a genuinely successful life. In fact, I believe it's the only way to bring real purpose into your life and to understand what genuine success really means.

"To find your mission in life," wrote author and Christian minister Frederick Buechner, "is to discover the intersection between your heart's deep gladness and the world's deep hunger." For me, that intersection defines the meaning of true success, which is, I believe, the point where your passions, values, talents, and dreams fall into alignment with the genuine desire to make the world a better place to live for all of its inhabitants. The interesting thing about this definition is that it not only describes the condition of success, it tells you exactly what you need to do to achieve it. Against the backdrop of the materialistic, winner-take-all mentality that pervades so many of our lives, it may seem counterintuitive, even naive, to believe that our own personal success can be enhanced by focusing on something other than competitive self-interest. But I know this to be true. Owning up to your responsibilities as a citizen of the planet, even in modest ways, generates a sense of purpose and power in your life that is the real engine behind genuine success. It taps your deepest potential and connects you to the bottomless reserves of commitment, perseverance, creativity, and hope that can make even the most extraordinary dreams come true.

And in the end, that's the message I want to leave with those students at Harvard and with you: The best way to live your life is with the assumption that your purpose on the planet is to strive, in some way appropriate to your means and your talents, to make a difference. To save, in essence, a little part of the world. An impossible notion? Perhaps. But an impossible notion is just an idea no one has had the guts to try. It's impossible, for example, to think that you can change troubled lives with something as fragile as an orchid, as spontaneous as jazz, as ephemeral as sunlight, or as unapologetically beautiful as a fountain or a well-proportioned space. And it's impossible to believe that the way to transform the life of a desperate young man and set him on a path that would lead to a life of remarkable experience, surprising achievement, resounding validation, and a deep and defining sense of purpose would be to sit him down at a potter's wheel and let him lay his hands on a spinning ball of raw, wet clay. Unless, of course, you learn to hear the voice that speaks from all of our hearts and tells us that it isn't.

INDEX

Alberti, Leon Battista, 142
Alcoa Corporation, 3
Alexander, Jane, 197
Alexander, Monte, 183
Allegheny County Airport, 149–51
Allis-Chalmers Corporation, 33
Alticor (Amway), 207
Amazon.com, 121
Appleyard, Robert, 55, 59, 157, 160
Ashby, Marty, 182–84, 191–93, 213–17
Astorino, Lou, 134–35

Bank of New York, 163
Bayer, 3–4, 23, 97–98, 189–90
Bayview Hunters Point Center for Arts
    and Technology (BAYCAT), San
    Francisco, 197–208
Beethoven, Ludwig von, 138
Benson, George, 180
Benzing, Peter, 98
Bey, Sharif, 18–20
Bezos, Jeff, 121
Biddle, Toby, 55, 57
Bidwell Presbyterian Church, 73
Bidwell Training Center, 2, 72–88,
    93, 158, 159–60, 216. See also
    Manchester Bidwell Center
Blakey, Art, 179
Blue Cross of Western Pennsylvania, 129
Braniff Airlines, 154
Brown, Ray, 180, 183

Brown, Willie, 197, 204
Brubeck, Dave, 23
Buechner, Frederick, 226
Burrell, Kenny, 183
Bush, George H. W., 174

Campbell, Joseph, 176
Carnegie, Andrew, 160
Carter, Lee, 206
Castellini, Bob, 207
Castellini Company, 207
Children's Hospital, Cincinnati,
    Ohio, 206
Chiron, 121
Cincinnati Center for Arts and
    Technology, 206–8
Clarke, Kenny, 179–80
Clinton, Hillary, 4
Concord Records, 213
Conrad, Ed, 82
Costa Rica, 209
Count Basie Orchestra, The, 4, 191
Cox, Tom, 54–58, 160
Csikszentmihalyi, Mihaly, 176,
    186–87
Culinary Institute of America, 24, 97
Cushing, Val, 100

DADC, 190
DeVos family, 207
Dix, Jim, 60

Index

D'Rivera, Paquito, 191
Duranty, Edmond, 145

Eastwood, Clint, 174
eBay, 202, 222
Eckstine, Billy, 180
Einstein, Albert, 138, 139
Eisner, Michael, 1
Ellington, Duke, 179, 211–13
Emery, Stewart, 119–20
Evans, Dwight, 94

Fast Company magazine, 197, 207
Fernandez, Ben, 99
Fife, Jesse, 77–78, 83–84, 86, 89–90, 92,
    128–29, 159, 167, 216–17
Fifth Third Bank, 207
Fox Chapel, Pennsylvania, 60
Frankl, Viktor, 114–15, 126–27

Galileo, 138
Garner, Erroll, 179
Getz, Stan, 105, 111
Giant Eagle, 136
Gillespie, Dizzy, 23, 102–4, 105,
    114, 183
Grameen Bank Project, 120–21

Hackett, Jim, 207
Hanks, Nancy, 174
Harper, Walt, 173–74, 175
Harvard Business School, 1, 5–6, 15,
    136, 220, 227
Heinz, John, 96
Heinz Corporation, 3, 24, 96
Heinz Foundation, 96, 97
Hero, Peter, 203
Heskett, Jim, 1, 5–6, 12, 13–14, 220
Hewlett-Packard, 3, 21
Hillman, Elsie, 96
Hines, Earl, 179
Hmong people, 13

IBM, 3, 82–84
Ikemoto, Howard, 140
Irvis, K. Leroy, 92–93, 94–95, 216

Jackson, Milt, 23
Jamal, Ahmad, 179
Jamison, Judith, 174
Jannetta, Diana, 91–92
Jobim, Antonio Carlos, 105
Jones, James Earl, 174
Jones, Quincy, 223

Kappmeyer, Keith, 129
Katselas, Tasso, 88–89, 181
Kaufmann, Edgar, 112–13, 164
King, Martin Luther, Jr., 7, 49, 50, 123

Lao-Tzu, 138–39
Lear, Norman, 213–14, 223
Lieberman, Bill, 93–94
Ligonier, Pennsylvania, 55–58, 70–71,
    101
Lins, Ivan, 4

MacArthur Foundation, 4, 11, 100,
    137–38, 197
Macy's Department Store, 224–25
Manchester Bidwell Center, 203–4;
    Amish quilts at, 13–14; architect for,
    12, 88–89, 181; architecture and
    concept for, 12–13, 87–89; ceramics
    studio, 21, 99–100, 192; chem tech
    lab and program, 22–23, 98, 189–90;
    concert hall, 179–84; corporate
    partnerships, 3–4, 21, 23, 24, 91,
    96–98, 134, 136, 189–90; culinary
    arts program, 24, 96–97, 144–45,
    171, 192; digital arts curriculum, 21,
    99; expansion into national and
    global centers, 194–218; fountain,
    24–25; George Nakashima furniture,
    13, 17; gourmet food, 24, 192;
    greenhouse, 25, 128–37, 145–46,
    166–67; groundbreaking, 95; Hmong
    "story cloth," 13; horticultural
    program, 25, 135–36, 192; jazz
    concert series, 4, 23–24, 103, 143,
    182–84, 216; Jesse Fife as COO,
    128–29; MCG Jazz, 4–5, 143,
    190–92, 193–94, 213–14; medical

coding program, 98; as model for national/global centers, 194–218; pharmacy tech program, 98; philosophy, 100, 117, 122–23, 178, 204, 207, 209, 221; photography program, 21–22, 99, 192; political support, 92–96; recipe for success, 3; size, 9; slide presentation, 1–27; staffing, 214–18; Strickland as CEO, 2, 9, 156; Strickland's vision, 81, 84–85, 87–91, 95, 97, 158; student body, 16, 100; success stories, 18–26, 143–45

Manchester Craftsmen's Guild, 2, 6–9, 60–65, 89, 91, 100, 142, 147, 166; operating budget, 60, 68; photography program, 68; Strickland as founder and director, 6–9, 55–65, 72, 73, 76, 154, 157, 160, 166, 173; success and expansion, 68–71, 99–100

Mangione, Chuck, 23

Man's Search for Meaning (Frankl), 114

Maslow, Abraham, 176

Mathieson, Drew, 160–64

MCG Jazz, 4, 24, 190–92, 213–14; Grammy Awards, 4–5, 24, 143, 191, 192, 193–94

McGuinn, Marty, 134, 163–64

McRae, Carmen, 105, 183

Mellon Bank, 134, 136, 160, 163–64, 190

Michelangelo, 138, 139

Montgomery, Wes, 105

Mr. Rogers' Neighborhood, 123

Mylan Labs, 4, 23, 98

Nakashima, George, 13

National Center for Arts and Technology, 209

National Council on the Arts, 4, 174–75

National Endowment for the Arts, 4, 174, 197

New York Voices, 4, 191

Nkubana, Janet, 224–25

Noble, Lee, 98

North Side Christian Ministry, 54

Nova Chemicals, 4, 23

Oprah Winfrey Show, The, 193–94

Parker, Charlie, 107–9

Parks, Gordon, 100

Pastore, John, 124–25

Penhoet, Ed, 121

Pennsylvania Arts Council, 91

Picasso, Pablo, 139, 139n

Pittsburgh, Pennsylvania: Bidwell Training Center, 72–88; closing of Allis-Chalmers, 33; Duquesne Club, 160–64; Episcopal Churches of, 7, 54–61, 68; highway bypass, 33–34; Hmong community, 13; jazz in, 179–80; Manchester neighborhood, 6, 32–35, 58; Oliver High School, 15–16, 28, 39–44, 48, 100–101, 172, 210; Phipps Conservatory, 129–30; poverty in, 28–30, 48, 49, 63–64, 187–88; public pool rescue, 225; race riots, 50–52; Strickland seeks funding, 79, 85; Symphony Orchestra, 182; Three Rivers Arts Festival, 47; Urban Renewal Authority, 134. *See also* Manchester Bidwell Center.

Porras, Jerry, 119–20

PPG Industries, 3

President's Committee on the Arts and Humanities, 4

Procter & Gamble, 207

Prudhomme, Paul, 24, 97

Purcell, John, 94

Reagan, Ronald, 85

Reed, Smith, Shaw & McClay, 59–60, 157

Reitz, Don, 100

Roach, Max, 183

Robinson, James, 73

Rogers, Fred, 123–25

Romoff, Jeff, 133, 136

Ross, Frank, 6–7, 39–49, 54, 59, 61, 62,

Ross, Frank (cont.)
   67, 69, 70, 85, 101, 105, 110–11, 112,
   148, 162, 166, 172, 178, 210

St. Michael's Parish, 57, 60, 70–71
Santorum, Rick, 4, 131–32, 135, 166–67
Schuller, Robert, 5
Shalit, Willa, 224
Shapira, David, 136
Silicon Valley Community Foundation,
   199–201, 203
Skoll, Jeff, 201–5, 209–10, 222
Skoll Community Fund, 202, 205
Smith, Max, 57–58
Sony Corporation, 190
Staton, Dakota, 180
Steelcase Corporation, 207
Strayhorn, Billy, 179, 211–13
Strickland, Bill, 77; appearance, 64, 163,
   167–69; as ceramics artist, 6–7,
   39–49, 70; choice about alcohol,
   126–27; Episcopal Church alliance,
   54–61; as founder and CEO of
   Manchester Bidwell Center, 2, 9, 156;
   founds Manchester Craftsmen's
   Guild, 6–9, 55–65, 68–71, 72, 73, 76,
   147, 166, 173; Frank Lloyd Wright
   and, 12, 61, 87, 88, 100, 112–14, 164;
   Frank Ross and, 6–7, 39–44, 46–49,
   54, 59, 61, 62, 67, 69, 70, 85, 100–101,
   105, 110–11, 112, 148, 162, 166, 172,
   178, 210; growing up poor, 28–32,
   35–39, 61–62; head of Bidwell
   Training Center, 72–88, 158, 159–60;
   jazz and, 102–14, 143, 148, 172–92,
   212–14; MacArthur Foundation
   genius grant, 4, 11, 100, 137–38, 197;
   Mellon Bank and, 163–64; mentors,
   157, 160–64, 167; on National
   Council on the Arts, 4, 174–75; on
   National Endowment for the Arts, 4,
   197; at Oliver High, 15, 28, 39–44,
   48, 100–101, 172; orchids and,
   129–31; passion for flying, 147–55,
   158, 196, 219; President's Committee
   on the Arts and Humanities, 4;
   speaking at Harvard Business School,

1–27; teaching aspirations, 54,
   142–43; tutoring in Manchester, 54;
   University of Pittsburgh student, 4,
   7, 48–49, 52–54, 65–67, 70, 142; University of Pittsburgh trustee, 4; vision
   for center, 81, 84–85, 87–91, 95, 97,
   104, 158, 196; vision for greenhouse,
   128–37, 145–46, 166, 196; vision for
   national/global centers, 194–218
Strickland, Evelyn, 35–39, 80, 162, 192
Strickland, William, Sr., 36–38, 47,
   61–62, 192
Success Built to Last (Porras et al.), 119–20

Tait, Gabe, 22
Taylor, Billy, 23, 172–75, 191–92
Thompson, Mark, 119–20
Thornburgh, Dick, 92, 181, 182
Thrift Drugs, 98
Tresvant, Linda, 206
Turrentine, Stanley, 179

University of Pittsburgh, 4, 7, 48–49,
   52–54, 65–67, 70, 142; Medical
   Center (UPMC), 133–34, 135, 136

Van Gogh, Vincent, 141–42
Verschell, Dick, 43–44

Welsh, Jim, 207
Werner, George, 59
West Michigan Center for Arts and
   Technology, 207
Western Pennsylvania Orchid Society,
   135
White, Dick, 98
Whole Foods, 136
Williams, Joe, 23
Williams, Mary Lou, 179
Wilson, Nancy, 4, 23, 105, 191, 193–94,
   223
Wishart, Alfred W. "Burr," 97
Wright, Frank Lloyd, 12, 61, 87, 88–89,
   98, 164; Fallingwater, 87, 101,
   112–14, 123, 164–65

Yunus, Muhammad, 120–21, 224